The Thirty-Six Strategies of Ancient China

三十六計

Stefan H. Verstappen

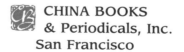

CHINA BOOKS
& Periodicals, Inc.
San Francisco

China Books & Periodicals, Inc.
2929 Twenty-Fourth Street
San Francisco, CA 94110

www.chinabooks.com

First Edition 1999

Book Design by Linda Revel
Cover Design by Stefan H. Verstappen & Linda Revel
Illustrations by Stefan H. Verstappen

Library of Congress Catalog Card Number: 99-72510

ISBN: 0-8351-2642-0

Printed in Canada

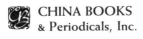 **CHINA BOOKS**
& Periodicals, Inc.

The Thirty-Six Strategies
of Ancient China

INTRODUCTION

The THIRTY-SIX STRATEGIES is a unique collection of ancient Chinese proverbs that describe some of the most cunning and subtle war tactics ever devised. Whereas other Chinese military texts such as Sun Zi's THE ART OF WAR focus on military organization, leadership, and battlefield tactics, the THIRTY-SIX STRATEGIES are more suitably applied in the fields of politics, diplomacy, and espionage. These proverbs describe not only battlefield strategies, but tactics used in psychological warfare to undermine both the enemy's will to fight and his sanity. Tactics such as the 'double cross,' the 'frame job,' and the 'bait and switch,' can be traced back through thousands of years of Chinese history to such proverbs as *Hide the Dagger Behind a Smile, Kill With a Borrowed Sword,* and *Toss Out a Brick to Attract Jade,* respectively. Though other Chinese military works of strategy have at least paid lip service to the Confucian notion of honor, the THIRTY-SIX STRATEGIES make no pretense of being anything but ruthless.

For the Western reader the THIRTY-SIX STRATEGIES offers timeless insights into the workings of human nature under conditions of extreme stress. Many of the proverbs are based on events that occurred during

China's Warring States Period (403-221 B.C.). This was a time so infamous that a later emperor banned history books of that era on the grounds that they contained accounts of such a devious nature, they would morally corrupt all who read them. Many of those accounts are presented here along with the exploits of some of the Orient's greatest generals, kings, emperors, and shoguns. Over 118 anecdotes are included to both explain and offer examples of each strategy's application. By learning from the old masters of the art of deception, one is better able to spot the modern pretenders, for, though the players come and go, the game remains the same.

HISTORY OF THE THIRTY-SIX STRATEGIES

The origin of the THIRTY-SIX STRATEGIES are unknown. No author or compiler has ever been mentioned, and no date as to when it may have been written has been ascertained. The first historical mention of the THIRTY-SIX STRATEGIES dates back to the Southern Qi dynasty (A.D. 489-537) where it is mentioned in the Nan Qi Shi (History of the Southern Chi Dynasty). It briefly records, "Of the 36 stratagems of Master Tan, running away is the best." Master Tan may be the famous General Tan Daoji (d. A.D. 436), but there is no evidence to either prove or disprove his authorship. While this is the first recorded mention of THIRTY-SIX STRATEGIES, some of the proverbs themselves are based on events that occurred up to seven hundred years earlier. For example, the strategy *Openly Repair the Walkway, Secretly March to Chencang* is based on a tactic allegedly used by the founder of the Han dynasty, Gaozu, to escape from Sichuan in 223 B.C. The strategy *Besiege Wei to Rescue Zhao* is named after an incident that took place even earlier, in 352 B.C., and is attributed to the famous strategist Sun Bin.

All modern versions of the THIRTY-SIX STRATEGIES are derived from a tattered book discovered at a roadside vendor's stall in Sichuan in 1941. It turned out to be a reprint of an earlier book dating back to the late Ming or early Qing dynasty entitled, THE SECRET ART OF WAR, THE THIRTY-SIX STRATEGIES. There was no mention of who the authors or compilers were or when it was originally published. A reprint was first published for the general public in Beijing in 1979. Since then several Chinese and English language versions have been published in China, Hong Kong, and Taiwan.

Without any other information, current speculations about the origin of the THIRTY-SIX STRATEGIES suggest that there was no single author. More likely the book derived from a collection of idiomatic expressions taken from popular Chinese folklore, history, and myths. They may have first been recorded by General Tan and handed down verbally or in manuscript form for centuries. It is believed that sometime in the early Qing dynasty some enterprising editor collected them and published them in the form that comes down to us today.

NOTES ON THE TEXT

The original text of THE SECRET ART OF WAR, THE THIRTY-SIX STRATEGIES is rather short, comprising only 138 Chinese characters. It merely names each strategy followed by a brief explanation. The book was divided into six categories of six strategies each. The six categories are said to correspond to six situations as follows: Stratagems when in a superior position; Stratagems for confrontation; Stratagems for attack; Stratagems for confused situations; Stratagems for gaining ground; and Stratagems for desperate situations. This division is based on the hexagrams of the I-CHING (a hexagram being a grouping of six broken or unbroken lines). In addition, the explanation of each strategy is likewise said to be based on the interpretation of each hexagram as found in the I-CHING. Initially all this seemed to imply an almost scientific approach, but on closer examination I found the structure flawed. My guess is that elements of I-CHING numerology were added at some time merely to create an aura of mystery and antiquity (not an uncommon practice among publishers during the Ming and Qing dynasties). Since the six subtitles did little to improve understanding, I did not use them in compiling the present text, but kept to the original sequence of strategies.

I used anecdotes primarily from both China's and Japan's 'Warring States' eras, since, though separated by more than a thousand years, those eras most closely reflected the tone of the strategies. My apologies to serious scholars for I rewrote the explanations and historical anecdotes so that they would be clearer to Western readers. Any mistakes and errors are my own. I also added opening quotes from other Oriental works on strategy, and a summary. The resultant manuscript is not a direct translation, nor a list of historical facts, but rather a retelling of Chinese folklore, or more specifically military lore

TABLE OF CONTENTS

CHAPTER ONE

第 一 計

瞞 天 過 海

FOOL THE EMPEROR TO CROSS THE SEA

In conflicts which involve large numbers of people, it is possible to get the opponent to become lax in their guard. When they are in a state of agitation and show signs of impatience, appear as if nothing is bothering you and put forth an easygoing, relaxed stance. When you perceive that the mood has been transferred (to your opponent), you have a chance to achieve victory by making a strong attack with as much speed as possible.

—MIYAMOTO MUSASHI

Moving about in the darkness and shadows, occupying isolated places, or hiding behind screens will only attract suspicious attention. To lower an enemy's guard you must act in the open, hiding your true intentions under the guise of common every day activities.[1]

WARRING STATES PERIOD CHINA

In 225 B.C. the state of Qin, having slowly increased its power over the past hundred years, now felt powerful enough to overcome its remaining opponents in open aggression. The most powerful of the remaining states was Chu. The king of Qin sent his renowned general Wang Jian to attack and conquer Chu. A year earlier Qin had sent another general, Li Xing, who suffered a humiliating defeat at the hands of Chu. The older and more experienced general Wang Jian wasn't going to make the same mistake as his predecessor and decided against invading the country directly. Instead he stopped just inside Qin's border with Chu and built a fortified stockade. The king of Chu called upon his allies to muster all available troops and rush them to the opposite side of the border. Confident from their previous victory, the Chu commanders rode out each day to challenge Wang to come out and fight, but Wang ignored the taunts. Instead Wang was observed swimming with his men in nearby rivers and lakes, or on leisurely picnics in the forest. At night there was feasting with singing and dancing. In addition Wang focused his efforts on improving the morale and training of his troops.

After several months the Chu army was beginning to grow weary of the game. One of the Chu commanders said, "Wang Jian has been sent to attack Chu, but it seems he is getting too old and he no longer has the heart for it. It is obvious that he has no intention of

---

1. The origin of this strategy is said to come from an incident involving the Tang dynasty emperor Tai Zong. The emperor was on campaign against the Koreans. His general advised crossing the Yellow Sea to the Korean Peninsula so that they would be able to surprise the Koreans from behind their lines. The plan had only one flaw—the Emperor was deathly afraid of large bodies of water. The generals devised a scheme where they decorated a large ship like a country estate and had banners hung all round so that you could not

attacking, but is here merely to save face." Others agreed and many of the troops were sent back to their countries. Wang Jian had waited behind his stockade almost an entire year before the last of the Chu troops also gave up waiting for his attack and broke camp to return to the capital. It was then that Wang ordered his men to suddenly sally forth and attack the retreating Chu. Because a retreating army is vulnerable to attack, coupled with the element of surprise, the Chu suffered severe losses and its general was slain. The king of Chu wasn't able to reassemble all his remaining troops in time, as Wang Jian swiftly invaded and conquered the entire kingdom. Four years later the king of Qin became the first emperor of China, Qin Shihuangdi.[2]

WARRING STATES PERIOD CHINA

General Li Mu was given the command responsible for defending Yanmen against the Xiongnu[3] who were constantly raiding the territories. When Li Mu first arrived at his new command everyone expected him to begin by launching attacks on the local tribes. But he did no such thing. Instead he focused his efforts on training and nurturing the border troops, ensuring they were well fed and paid. He further ordered that, should the Xiongnu attack, all troops were to retreat into one of the fortified towns that were scattered throughout the countryside and merely defend. Under no circumstances were they to engage the enemy. For several

---

see the ocean. They then told the emperor that a local aristocrat cordially invited the Emperor to dine at his estate. Once aboard, the emperor was dined and entertained throughout the night while the ship silently set sail. The next morning they arrived at their destination with the emperor none the wiser.

2. From RECORDS OF THE GRAND HISTORIAN.

3. Nomadic horsemen that occupied the central Asian steppes to the north and west of China.

years, anytime a Xiongnu raiding party entered the territory they found the people and soldiers already holed-up behind defensive walls with precious little left in the countryside to plunder. Eventually the Xiongnu and even Li Mu's own soldiers thought that, though he was a virtuous commander, he was also a coward. The border troops, after years of training without engaging in battle, became restless for combat. When Li Mu saw the eagerness for battle amongst his troops he decided to act. First he sent his best troops to set up an ambush several days march away. Then he had herds of cattle and their drivers released to graze in the fields with only a few soldiers to watch over them. When a Xiongnu raiding party happened upon the cattle they attacked and sent the soldiers fleeing. The raiding party sent word back to their Khan that the Chinese had abandoned the country leaving herds of cattle and lightly defended villages behind. The Khan raised a tremendous host to invade the Chinese territory. Expecting no resistance from the 'cowardly' Li Mu, they were easily led into the ambush. More than a hundred thousand Xiongnu horsemen were killed. For ten years thereafter, not a single raiding party dared cross the border.[4]

JAPANESE FOLK TALE

There once lived a samurai who was plagued by a large and clever rat who had the run of the house. This annoyed the samurai to no end so he went to the village to buy a cat. A street vendor sold him a cat that he said would catch the rat, and indeed the cat looked trim and fit. But the rat was even quicker than the cat and after a week with no success the samurai returned the cat. This time the vendor pulled out a large and grizzled cat and guaranteed that no rat could escape this master mouser.

---

4. From UNORTHODOX STRATEGIES.

The rat knew enough to stay clear of this tough alley cat, but when the cat slept, the rat ran about. Half the day the rat would hide, but the other half he again had the run of the place. The samurai brought the cat back to the vendor who shook his head in despair saying he had given the samurai his best cat and there was nothing more he could do. Returning home with his money, the samurai happened upon a monk and sought his advice. After hearing the samurai's story the monk offered him the services of the cat that lived in the temple. The cat was old and fat and he scarcely seemed to notice when he was carried away by the doubtful samurai. For two weeks the cat did little more than sleep all day and night. The samurai wanted to give the cat back to the temple but the monk insisted he keep him a while longer assuring him the rat's days were close to an end. The rat became accustomed to the presence of the lazy old cat and was soon up to his old tricks even, on occasion, brazenly dancing around the old cat as he slept. Then one day, as the rat went about his business without any concern, he passed close by the cat who swiftly struck out his paw and pinned the rat to the floor. The rat died instantly.[5]

SUMMARY

In battle, the element of surprise is paramount. A wary opponent is unlikely to fall into the usual traps, so he must first be made to relax his vigilance. To do this one must carry on as though nothing untoward was afoot. Once acclimatized to often repeated actions, a person no longer takes notice of them.[6] When the enemy ceases to pay attention to you, the time is right to attack.

5. From THE ZEN WAY TO THE MARTIAL ARTS.

6. In Psychology this phenomenon is known as habituation: the more often you are exposed to a stimulus, the less sensitive you become to it.

CHAPTER TWO

圍魏救趙

BESIEGE WEI TO RESCUE ZHAO

Attack where he is unprepared,
appear where unexpected.

—SUN ZI

When the enemy is too strong to attack directly, then attack something he holds dear. Know that in all things he cannot be superior. Somewhere there is a gap in the armor, a weakness that can be attacked instead. If the enemy is on campaign, his home defense will be weak, if his army is fast, his baggage trains will be slow, if the army well equipped, the treasury will be at a loss.[1]

---

1. During the incessant feuding between the various kingdoms of the Warring States Period, any kingdom that attacked another was in danger of being attacked by a third country from the rear. This strategy was used to maintain a certain degree of military status quo. If any one kingdom attacked another, the rest would sit back and watch the outcome. But if it looked as though one kingdom was going to become too powerful, then the other kingdoms would unite to cut the ambitious state back down to size. This went on for several hundred years, but in the end the Warring States rulers

WARRING STATES PERIOD CHINA

This strategy derives its name from a famous incident that occurred in 354 B.C. At this time one of China's most renowned strategists, Sun Bin, (a descendent of Sun Zi) was an advisor to the king of Qi. Sun had earlier been at the court of Wei, but another minister, Pang Juan, became jealous of Sun's cleverness. Through court intrigues he had Sun framed as a spy, sentenced to mutilation, and imprisoned. Sun escaped (see Chapter 27) and fled to Qi. Several years later the king of Wei appointed the same Pang Juan as commander of the army and sent him to attack the capital of Zhao. The king of Zhao immediately appealed to Qi for help. The king of Qi consulted his advisors who all spoke in favor of rushing to aid their ally, only Sun Bin recommended against attacking. Sun advised, "To intervene between two warring armies is like trying to divert a tidal wave by standing in its path. It would be better to wait until both armies have worn themselves out." The king agreed to wait.

The siege of Zhao had lasted more than a year when Sun Bin decided the time was ripe to come to Zhao's aid. The king of Qi appointed Prince Tian Ji as general and Sun as military advisor. Tian Ji wanted to attack the Wei forces directly to lift the siege of Zhao, but again Sun advised against direct intervention saying, "Since most of Wei's troops are out of the country engaged in the siege, their own defense must be weak. By attacking the capital of Wei, we will force the Wei

---

neglected this strategy and the kingdom of Qin was finally able to conquer all of China.

2. From THE ART OF WARFARE by Sun Bin. Another variation of the story is found in the ZHAN GUO CE, though the minister credited with the strategy is not Sun Bin, but Tuan-kan Lun.

3. Approximately 0.3 miles.

army to return to defend their own capital thereby lifting the siege of Zhao while destroying the Wei forces in turn." Tian Ji agreed to the plan and divided his army into two parts, one to attack the capital of Wei, and the other to prepare an ambush along the route to the capital.

When the Wei general Pang Juan heard that the capital was being attacked, he rushed his army back to its defense. Weakened and exhausted from the year-long siege and the forced march, the Wei troops were completely caught by surprise in the ambush and suffered heavy losses. Zhao was thus rescued while Pang Juan barely escaped back to Wei to recoup his losses. Sun Bin would later defeat his nemesis Pang Juan using another classic strategy (see Chapter 28).[2]

HAN DYNASTY CHINA

After having defeated Wei, the Han general, Han Xin, led his army through the Jing River gorge to subdue Zhao. The king of Zhao in turn mobilized his army and set up fortified positions just in front of the mouth of the gorge where the Han army would have to exit. Han Xin, knowing the most logical place for an ambush would be at the exit, halted his army some thirty li[3] from the mouth. During the night Han Xin ordered two thousand of his light cavalry to muffle their horse's hooves and secretly make their way through underbrush to set up an observation post overlooking the enemy's encampment. Each man was furthermore instructed to carry a red flag. Han Xin told his commanders, "When the Zhao forces see me march out, they are sure to abandon their fortifications and come in pursuit. Then you must enter their walls with all speed, tear down the Zhao flags, and set up the red flags of Han instead." The next day Han Xin ordered the main body of his army to line up with their backs against the river. When the Zhao troops saw this they rejoiced in their assured victory since it was a well known rule of war to never fight with water at your back. Han Xin moved first, launching an attack against the Zhao positions. After a while the Han feigned a retreat and fled back to the main body still lined up along the river. The Zhao forces, feeling confident in their advantage of terrain and superior numbers, pursued the Han to the river where they engaged in a fierce battle. As Han Xin had anticipated, the Zhao forces completely abandoned their camp leaving only a handful of soldiers behind. When the Han cavalrymen hiding in the mountains saw the Zhao army deserting their camp, they knew the time had come. They charged down the mountain, entered the compound and quickly killed the remaining Zhao guards. Then they tore down the Zhao banners and replaced them with the red flags of Han. Meanwhile, the Zhao forces were unable to gain any advantage in the desperate fighting along the river, and so were about to retreat to their camp when they saw the Han flags flying behind the ramparts. The Zhao soldiers, believing that the Han had already captured their leaders, panicked and fled in all directions to escape. The Han then closed in from both the river and the camp to attack on two fronts, inflicting a severe defeat and capturing the king of Zhao.[4]

WARRING STATES PERIOD CHINA

Duke Wen of Qin had decided to invade Wei, so he called in the feudal nobles to lay out his plans for attack. However he was interrupted by the laughter coming from one of the nobles named Kong Zichu.

"May I ask the source of your amusement?" asked the duke.

---

4. From RECORDS OF THE GRAND HISTORIAN.

"I was laughing at a man in my neighborhood and some gossip I heard," replied Kong.

"It seems one day he was walking home with his wife when he spotted a lovely maiden gathering mulberry leaves by the roadside. No sooner did he escape his wife to go flirt with the girl when, upon turning around, he saw another man making love to his wife. I was just thinking about the story and I couldn't help but laugh."

Seeing the moral of this story Duke Wen canceled his invasion plans and recalled his army from its march. No sooner had the Qin army returned when they were sent out to stop an invasion on their own northern border by an unexpected enemy.[5]

SUMMARY

To confront a powerful opponent in a head to head contest of strength is the most costly and least favorable method of war. Instead, while the enemy is preoccupied with other objectives you attack something of value that he has left behind unguarded. When he is forced to break off his current campaign in order to rescue what he has lost, you can lead his disheartened forces into a trap.

---

5. From the ZHAN GUO CE.

CHAPTER THREE

KILL WITH A
BORROWED SWORD

If you are limited in your own strength, then borrow the strength of the enemy. If you cannot neutralize an enemy, borrow an enemy's knife to do so. If you have no generals, borrow those of the enemy.

—SUN ZI

When you do not have the means to attack your enemy directly, then attack using the strength of another. Trick an ally into attacking him, bribe an official to turn traitor, or use the enemy's own strength against him.[1]

SPRING AND AUTUMN PERIOD CHINA

The duke of Zheng wanted to invade the state of Kuai. To prepare for his invasion he first sent out spies to find out who were the most capable military advisors at the

---

1. Quote from THE CORE OF THE ART OF WAR—the long lost chapters from Sun Zi's THE ART OF WAR recently recovered from a Han dynasty tomb.

Kuai court. Once he had a list of names, the duke had a rumor spread among his troops saying that victory was assured since he had Kuai's best generals secretly on his side. He also had a decree drawn up promising these generals that, once he had conquered Kuai, they would all be richly rewarded with titles and territories. To back up his promise he had the decree enshrined in a local temple were everyone could see it. Naturally the king of Kuai had spies in Zheng's army and they reported the names of the alleged treacherous generals to the king. Believing his trusted advisors were preparing to betray him, the king of Kuai had them all executed. When the duke of Zheng heard of the executions, he launched his attack. The king of Kuai became alarmed at the sudden invasion of his territory and called his army staff together to mount a counter attack. But the recent executions had eliminated all his capable leaders. The remaining junior officers were inexperienced and unsure of how to respond. Their hesitation cost the king his throne, and his head.[2]

WARRING STATES PERIOD CHINA

Chang Tuo defected from Western Zhou and went to Eastern Zhou where he revealed all of Western Zhou's state secrets. Eastern Zhou rejoiced while Western Zhou was furious. Minister Feng Chu said to the king of Western Zhou, "I can assassinate that man if your highness will give me thirty catties of gold." The king consented and the next day Feng Chu sent an agent to the Eastern Zhou court bearing the gold and a letter addressed to Chang Tuo. The letter read, "This is to remind Chang Tuo that you must complete your mission as soon as possible, for the longer the delay the more likely you will be found out." However, before the first

---

2. From the ZUO ZHUAN.

agent departed, Feng Chu sent another agent to the Eastern Zhou border guards informing them that a spy would be crossing the border that night. When the first agent arrived at the border he was stopped and searched. The border guards found the gold and the letter to Chang Tuo and turned them over to their court officials. Shortly afterwards Chang Tuo was executed.[3]

CHINESE FOLK TALE

One day a fox was wandering through the woods preoccupied in thought when he was suddenly surprised by a tiger who seemed intent on eating him. It being too late to run away, the fox had to think quickly. Nonchalantly he asked, "Tiger why are you here, are you not afraid of me?"

"Why should I be afraid of you?" asked the tiger.

"Because I am the king of the jungle," said the fox.

"Ridiculous!" replied the Tiger. "I am king of the jungle."

"Well if you don't believe me I'll prove it. Just follow me as I walk about the jungle and see for yourself if the other animals do not run away at my approach."

The tiger agreed and so the fox set off with the tiger following closely behind. As the other animals spotted the fox they also saw the tiger and they ran away. After a while the fox turned to the tiger and said, "See how they scatter when I approach. Do you believe me now?"

"It seems I was wrong," said the perplexed Tiger, and he sulked away into the jungle.[4]

SUMMARY

To succeed in any endeavor one must be frugal in expending one's resources. Where possible, use trickery and deception to appropriate the strength of others while conserving your own.

---

3. From the ZHAN GUO CE.
4. Ibid.

CHAPTER FOUR

第四計

以逸待勞

AWAIT THE EXHAUSTED ENEMY AT YOUR EASE

Whoever is first in the field and awaits the coming of the enemy will be fresh for the fight, whoever is second in the field and has to hasten into formation will fight already exhausted.

—SUN ZI

It is an advantage to choose the time and place for battle. In this way you know when and where the battle will take place, while your enemy does not. Encourage your enemy to expend his energy in futile quests while you conserve your strength. When he is exhausted and confused, you attack with energy and purpose.

— 19 —

SPRING AND AUTUMN PERIOD CHINA

In 684 B.C. the state of Qi attacked the state of Lu. When the two armies met at Changshao, Duke Zhuang of Lu wanted to beat the drums and begin his advance, but he was dissuaded by his chief advisor Cao Gui who said, "Not yet."

Only after the Qi troops had beaten their drums three times did Cao cry, "Now is the time to beat ours!"

The Lu troops then charged and defeated the Qi. The duke was eager to pursue the retreating Qi troops when he was again stopped by Cao who said, "Not yet." Cao then dismounted his chariot and went to inspect the tracks made by the retreating Qi troops. When he climbed back aboard he said, "All right, lets pursue them." The Qi troops were thus driven out of the Lu territory.

After the victory was won the duke asked Cao Gui the reason for his actions, to which Cao Gui replied, "In battle, it is all a matter of morale. The first beating of the drum is to rouse the soldiers to action. If no action is taken, then, at the second beating, their morale begins to dwindle, and at the third it is gone. When the enemy was at the end of their enthusiasm, we were at the peak of ours. That is the time to attack. Because of this we were able to defeat them. But in dealing with seasoned generals it is often difficult to see through their tactics. I was therefore afraid that they might have made an ambush ready for us. But when I found that during their retreat their chariot tracks were disorderly and their banners discarded, I knew we could chase them out."[1]

SPRING AND AUTUMN PERIOD CHINA

In 628 B.C. the commander of a Qin division stationed in the capital of their ally, the state of Zheng, saw an opportunity to "lead a sheep away" and sent a message

---

1. From the ZUO ZHUAN.

to his ruler, Duke Mu. He reported that the Zheng officials had entrusted his division with the keys and defense of the north gate, therefore if the duke were to secretly send an army, the Qin garrison could attack from inside and open the gates, thus easily taking the city. Duke Mu consulted his advisor, Jian Shu, on his plan to secretly attack Zheng and the latter replied, "I have never heard of wearing out an army attempting to make a surprise attack on a distant state. If our army is worn out and its strength exhausted while the ruler of the distant state has prepared for our attack, will the outcome not be disaster? If our army knows where its going, certainly Zheng will find out as well, after traveling a thousand *li*, who could fail to guess our intentions?" But the Duke ignored this advice and ordered his troops to mobilize. As the army rode out the gate they passed the old advisor who stood weeping by the roadside. When asked why he was crying, Jian Shu replied, "I see the army marching out and my son with it, but I will see neither return. If Jin should decide to intervene they will intercept you at the Yao Pass. It is there that I shall go to retrieve your bones."

As the old advisor predicted, Zheng discovered the plot and the Qin collaborators fled to distant parts. When the Qin army arrived they discovered Zheng well prepared to meet them. Seeing no way to capture the capital, the Qin army turned for home stopping along the way to wipe out the small state of Hua. Meanwhile, in the state of Jin, which was an ally of the now defunct state of Hua, the commander Yuan Zhen was enraged by the actions of Qin. He said to the king, "Qin has ignored Jian Shu's advice and has worn out its people on a mission of greed. Heaven presents us with this opportunity, and an opportunity thus presented must not be lost! One must not allow the enemy to escape, for to do so means trouble in the future. We must attack the Qin army." The king was persuaded and the order was issued to attack. The Qin army was soundly defeated at the Yao Pass.[2]

CHINESE FOLK TALE

Emperor Xuan of Zhou loved to gamble on cock fights and kept a stable of specially bred fighting roosters. Although they were strong and fierce they would nevertheless lose against the roosters trained by Ji Xingze. The emperor therefore hired Ji to train his roosters.

Ten days had passed when the emperor went to the stables to ask if they were ready to fight.

"No," said Ji. "they are far too fierce and proud of their strength. They rush to attack even the slightest noise."

After another ten days passed the emperor returned to inquire again.

"Not yet. They are still haughty and jump at everything that moves."

After another ten days the emperor again asked the question.

"No, still not yet. Although they no longer rush to attack, they still raise their hackles and stare fiercely at the slightest provocation."

After yet another ten days the emperor again asked if the roosters were ready.

"Yes, they are nearly ready. Although some still crow from time to time, none ever change their countenance. From a distance they appear as steady is if they were made of wood. Before them, their untrained opponents would not dare accept their challenge and could only turn back and run."[3]

SUMMARY

While there are circumstances when it is necessary for an army to hurry to the battlefield in order to command the advantage of terrain, or weather, it is more often a mistake to rush to battle without a definite advantage for doing so.

---

2. From RECORDS OF THE GRAND HISTORIAN.
3. From Ancient Chinese Parables.

CHAPTER FIVE

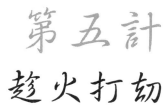

第五計

趁火打劫

LOOT A
BURNING HOUSE

Now, when your army is exhausted and your resources are spent, this is the time that new opponents enter the field to take advantage of your weakness. No matter how clever the leader is, once this situation has come about, the end is inevitable.

—SUN ZI

When a country is beset by internal conflicts, when disease and famine ravage the population, when corruption and crime are rampant, then it will be unable to deal with an outside threat. This is the time to attack.[1]

SPRING AND AUTUMN PERIOD CHINA

In the year 499 B.C. the king of Wu, Fu Chai, conquered the state of Yue and captured its king, Gou Jian. Rather than have him executed, the king of Wu made the deposed king of Yue work as a stable boy cleaning the

1. From the ZHAN GUO CE.

imperial stables. After three years the king of Wu was feeling quite invincible and released Gou Jian to return to his country to serve as a vassal to the state of Wu. Once back in his home country, Gou Jian set about rebuilding his economy and reputation. Through his benevolent rule the people prospered and upstanding counselors and commanders were drawn to his court to offer their services. After seven years of enlightened rule, Gou Jian knew that his citizens and his commanders would be willing to suffer even the hardships of war for his cause. To prepare for the impending attack on Wu, Gou Jian began with *The Strategy of Sowing Discord* (see Chapter 33). First, he bribed Wu's chief minister with eight beautiful women and a thousand pieces of gold. Next, he had false evidence planted against Wu's chief councilor who was thereby forced to commit suicide. Then fate provided Gou Jian with another strategy. That year Wu was experiencing a severe drought and the people were hungry. The king of Wu had spent copiously from his treasury in order to build a new palace and was reluctant to provide relief. Seizing the opportunity, Gou Jian sent a tribute consisting of a huge shipment of building materials with full honor guard in parade dress. This ostentatious display of wealth slowly wound its way through the hardest hit areas of the drought. The impoverished peasantry, seeing that the king was spending the treasury on lumber for his palace instead of rice for his starving subjects, began a revolt. The fatally arrogant king of Wu still balked at the earnest advice to send provisions to the drought ridden provinces, and sent out the army instead. This left the Wu capital poorly defended. As soon as his spies had reported on this, Guo Jian launched an attack on the capital of Wu. The king of Wu woke the next day to find his city surrounded and his army far away on campaign. Left with no able commanders and only the advice of the few ineffectual courtiers that survived his purges, the king fled into the countryside where he was dealt with later (see Chapter 22). Thus the king of Yue looted the burning house of Wu by setting the spark.[2]

WARRING STATES PERIOD CHINA

Qi and Han were allies when Zhang Yi attacked Han with the combined forces of Qin and Wei. Han asked Qi for assistance. The king of Qi said, "Han is our ally and since Qin has attacked her we must go to her rescue." But his minister Su Tianchen disagreed saying, "Your majesty's planning is faulty. You should merely agree to assist Han but take no action there. However, in the kingdom of Yan, their king has recently resigned the throne to his despised prime minister. This has enraged both the noble houses and the common people causing turmoil at court. Now, if Qin attacks Han, Chu and Zhao will surely come to her aid, and this will be as good as heaven bestowing Yan upon us."

The king approved and promised the Han envoy assistance before sending him back to Han believing he had Qi's backing. When Qin attacked Han, Chu and Zhao intervened as expected. While all the major kingdoms were thus engaged in the battle for Han, Qi stealthily attacked Yan. Within thirty days Yan was captured.[3]

SIX DYNASTIES PERIOD CHINA

It is written that King Hou Zhuwei of Northern Qi employed perverse sycophants to govern the realm and exercise control over planning. Each of these men in turn maintained their own personal factions, promoting their own cronies outside the normal order. The laws were relaxed, official matters advanced by wealth, lawsuits

2. From the ZHAN GUO CE.

3. From UNORTHODOX STRATEGIES.

were concluded through bribes, and chaotic government harmed the people. Subsequently these actions brought about the specter of drought and flooding rains, while raiders and thieves both increased. Moreover the ruler was suspicious and jealous of other kings so that they suffered harm even though they were innocent. Several high officials fell under suspicion and were executed even though they had not committed any crime. Gradually the signs of corruption and decay were being manifest so that the end was in sight. Shortly thereafter, the emperor Wu of Northern Zhou took advantage of the situation to attack and exterminate the kingdom of Northern Qi.[4]

SUMMARY

The death of every civilization is brought on by three events: starvation, disease, and war. A culture suffering from any two becomes the target for the third. An ancient proverb states that when a tiger is sick or wounded, jackals gather nearby.

4."Drought and rain" is a reference to the maintenance of China's dike and canal system which was the expensive and ongoing responsibility of the central government. If the government was lax in its maintenance and allowed the system to fall into disrepair, then irrigated areas would suffer drought while silt on the riverbed would build up until the river overflowed the dikes, flooding the lowlands. The degree to which this system was maintained was a considered an indicator of the stability of the government.

CHAPTER SIX

第六計

聲東擊西

CLAMOR IN THE EAST, ATTACK IN THE WEST

The spot where we intend to fight must not be made known, for then the enemy will have to prepare against a possible attack at different points and his forces will then be spread out too thin. For, if the enemy should strengthen his van, he will weaken his rear. Should he strengthen his rear, he will weaken his van.

—SUN ZI

In any battle the element of surprise can provide an overwhelming advantage. Even when face to face with an enemy, surprise can still be employed by attacking where he least expects it. To do this you must create an expectation in the enemy's mind through the use of a feint. If you plan to attack on the right flank, you first maneuver your left, if you wish to invade, you first pretend to improve your defense, if you intend to hold your ground, make a display of packing up.

THREE KINGDOMS PERIOD CHINA

In A.D. 200 rival warlords Yuan Shao and the infamous Cao Cao met at what would be the battle of Guandu. The numerically superior forces of Yuan Shao sent a division to attack the small city of Baima situated to the rear of Cao Cao's army. Yuan Shao hoped this maneuver would cut off his enemy's communications, supply lines, and avenue of escape, thus ending their long rivalry. When reports came in that Baima was under siege, Cao Cao called together his advisors to plan a way out of their precarious situation. They could not go directly to Baima since they would be vastly outnumbered, yet they could not allow Yuan Shao to occupy such a strategic position. Then one advisor suggested a feint against Yuan Shao's old stronghold at the city of Ye. Cao Cao agreed to this plan and personally led the army towards Ye. When Yuan Shao heard that Cao Cao had crossed the river and was heading towards Ye, he and half of his forces went with the intention of trapping Cao Cao between the Ye garrison in the front and his reinforcements from the rear.

Meanwhile, Cao Cao had reversed directions in the middle of the night and, through a forced march, arrived at Baima before dawn. There Yuan Shao's remaining troops were completely taken by surprise and annihilated using the very strategy Yuan Shao hoped to use at Ye. When Yuan Shao reached Ye, he found no one had seen nor heard of any invading army. Realizing he had been tricked, Yuan Shao turned his army around to return to Baima. On the way back, Yuan Shao learned that his general had been killed and the siege lifted. Realizing he had lost the engagement, Yuan Shao returned to his old stronghold of Ye to recoup his losses. But in the end he would lose all to China's most notoriously cunning strategist, Cao Cao.[1]

SONG DYNASTY CHINA

Once there was an official who was transferred to the capital. The front part of the inn where he stayed was a teahouse, and across the street was a shop that sold expensive dyed silks. Whenever he had nothing to do, he would sit at a table watching the people and activity on the street. One day he noticed with surprise that several suspicious looking characters were walking back and forth observing the silk shop with great interest. One of them came up to his table and whispered, "We're in the robbery business and we're here to steal those fine silks. Since you noticed us, I came to ask you not to mention it."

"That has nothing to do with me," the official replied. "Why should I say anything about it?"

The fellow thanked him and left. The official thought to himself, "The silk shop has its wares openly displayed on a busy street. In broad daylight, with a thousand eyes watching, if they have the skill to steal those silks, then they must be smart thieves indeed." So he watched carefully to see how they would manage it. But what he saw was only the same people walking back and forth in front of the silk shop. Sometimes they gathered on the left, sometimes on the right. The official sat watching until after sunset when everyone had gone and the shop had closed. "Those fools," said the official to himself. "They were putting one over on me." When he returned to his room to order some food, he discovered that all his belongings were gone.[2]

YUAN DYNASTY CHINA

In 1220 Genghis Khan and his general, Subede, were planning the conquest of the Muslim Empire of Shah

---

1. From ROMANCE OF THE THREE KINGDOMS.
2. From LIANGXI MANZHI, translated by Amy Ling.

Ala ed-Din Mohammed. After crossing the Pamirs Mountains, Genghis entered the eastern edges of the Shah's empire in the Fergana Valley where he split his army into three divisions. Two divisions continued west to attack Kokan. When the Shah heard that two Mongol columns were marching towards Kokan, he rushed all remaining reserves to secure this area. Meanwhile Genghis' own column quietly turned north and, in a legendary feat of endurance, crossed 300 miles through the reputedly impassable Kyzyl Kum Desert. Three months later they emerged at Bokhara, deep in the heart of the empire and well behind enemy lines. With no one to oppose them, Genghis' troops were able to cut the Shah's communications preventing him from calling in reserves and supplies from the western provinces. All three armies then converged on Samarkand. Mohammed, cut off from his reinforcements, realized the situation was hopeless and escaped to the south with his remaining troops. He lived as a fugitive being hunted by the Mongol forces from town to town until he died one year later.[3]

SUMMARY

Where the enemy expects you to attack, he will reinforce. When he does so, a part of his army is thus neutralized, defending nothing. Then, with your full strength, attack his remaining forces.

---

3. From THE MONGOL WARLORDS.

CHAPTER SEVEN

第七計

無中生有

CREATE SOMETHING FROM NOTHING

Turning back is how the Way moves; weakness is the means the Way employs. The myriad things in the world are born from Something, and Something from Nothing.

—LAO ZI

Use the same feint twice. Having reacted to the first and often the second feint as well, the enemy will be hesitant to react to a third feint. Therefore, the third feint is the actual attack catching your enemy with his guard down.

SIX DYNASTIES PERIOD CHINA

General He Ruodun of the Northern Zhou led his troops across the Yangtze to attack the state of Chen. General Hou Qi of Chen was sent forth to stop the Zhou invasion. Both armies set up fortified camps along opposite sides of the river. Shortly after arriving on the scene, heavy rains caused flooding which cut off the supply lines of the invading Zhou army. Their troops were forced to scavenge for supplies while the Chen troops had supplies ferried along the river in small river craft. General He knew that without supplies his army would be forced to retreat, so he sought to likewise cut the Chen supply lines. First he had several boats built to resemble the local style and late at night ferried them to the Chen encampment. Inside the boats were hidden heavily armed shock troops. When the Chen troops waded out to receive what they believed to be their supply boats, they were taken by surprise. The shock troops inflicted heavy casualties and captured several Chen soldiers to be brought back for interrogation. From these captured troops General He learned that several of his own troops had deserted by riding down river until they were picked up by the Chen patrol boats. To prevent further desertions, General He had some horses brought onto his boats and then whipped. After this was repeated several times the horses became deathly afraid of boats and would rear and kick whenever one came close. He then sent a light division down river to set up an ambush. Several soldiers were given the boat-shy horses and told to ride along the river and pretend to defect to the Chen side. When the Chen river patrol saw the potential deserters, they brought the boats to the shore to pick up the new recruits. But when the horses were being loaded on board, they reared and kicked. Distracted by the commotion, the Chen troops were surprised and killed by the Zhou troops waiting in ambush. Thereafter, anytime a boat came down river, the Chen forces would chase it away, fearing another ambush. And anytime they saw troops willing to desert, they would refuse, fearing another trap.[1]

SUI DYNASTY CHINA

In 587 the first Sui emperor, Wendi, launched an attack on the state of Chen. He sent one of his generals, He Nuobi, to encamp on the north side of the Yangtze River (which marked the boundary between the two kingdoms) opposite the enemy's capital. Now every general knows that to be

---

1. From UNORTHODOX STRATEGIES.

attacked while crossing a river is disastrous, so both camps waited for the other to make the first move. Each day He Nuobi ordered his troops to practice maneuvers and create a great deal of noise as though preparing for battle, but he did not cross the river. The first time this happened the Chen commanders were certain that the invasion had begun and they ordered their men to form defensive positions. But by sunset still no attack had come. Day after day this continued until finally the Chen general said, "That old fool is only playing games with us. We will pay no further attention to his antics." Meanwhile, General He Nuobi secretly bought or confiscated as many river boats as he could get hold of and had them hidden. Then he found a few dozen old hulks and used them to patrol the river. When the Chen patrols saw these wrecks they believed that the Sui army had, in any event, no usable boats with which to cross. By this time the Chen patrols ceased being on the alert. Having lowered the enemy's guard, General He Nuobi readied his hidden armada and prepared his men for battle. As a final precaution just before he launched his attack, he sent a group of soldiers disguised as hunters across the river to create a commotion by riding through the underbrush. The Chen troops were distracted by the sounds of the hunting party and failed to notice the Sui army crossing the river. The Chen forces were taken by surprise and all were put to the sword but one, who was allowed to escape to bring the news back to the capital. When the lone survivor gave his report, the king of Chen ordered his remaining troops to immediately set out for the border. He Nuobi had anticipated this move and had prepared an ambush that succeeded in wiping out the remaining Chen forces. When the Sui army arrived at the Chen capital, the king had no troops left with which to defend the city. The king was taken prisoner, and the state of Chen became a province of the Sui empire.[2]

---

2. From THE SUI DYNASTY.

TANG DYNASTY CHINA

During the An Lushan rebellion in A.D. 756 the Tang general Zhang Xun was under siege by the forces of General Linghu Chao. Outnumbered twenty to one, the defending Tang forces soon ran out of arrows. To remedy this General Zhang ordered his men to make straw dummies and dress them in black uniforms. That night the dummies were lowered over the city walls by ropes, accompanied to the beat of war drums and gongs. General Linghu thought the enemy was launching a surprise night offensive and ordered his archers to shower the figures descending the walls with arrows. Once the dummies where riddled with arrows the Tang soldiers pulled them back up over the walls, thus restoring their supply of arrows.

The next day General Linghu, feeling humiliated, attacked the walls in revenge. That night the Tang again lowered the dummies but General Linghu ordered his men to ignore them believing it was the same trick to get more arrows. When General Zhang saw that no one was firing at the straw dummies, he ordered five hundred of his best troops to be lowered instead. They made a lightning raid on the encamped soldiers, catching them completely by surprise. The siege was lifted and General Linghu's army fled the field.[3]

SUMMARY

Sun Zi wrote that the direct attack and the indirect attack are interchangeable depending on the enemy's expectation. Here a feint (Nothing) becomes the direct attack (Something) which, due to the enemy's assumptions, is in fact an indirect attack. This is what is meant by being interchangeable.

---

3. From THE IMPERIAL HISTORY OF CHINA.

CHAPTER EIGHT

第八計

暗渡陳倉

OPENLY REPAIR THE WALKWAY, SECRETLY MARCH TO CHENCANG

To win victory in battle, the leader must know how to use both direct and indirect methods. The interplay between direct and indirect methods generates countless tactics.

—SUN ZI

Attack the enemy with two convergent forces. The first is the direct attack, one that is obvious and for which the enemy prepares his defense. The second is the indirect attack, the attack sinister, that the enemy does not expect and which causes him to divide his forces at the last minute, leading to confusion and disaster.[1]

WARRING STATES PERIOD CHINA

In 270 B.C. the town of Ouyu, bordering the kingdom of Zhao, was besieged by Qin. The king of Zhao consulted his advisors, most of whom recommended against marching to save Ouyu, citing that the terrain was too rugged and difficult to cross. Only Zhao She suggested an attack regardless of the terrain. He said, "Qin is unsure whether we will attack since Ouyu is on the far border of our territory with difficult terrain between us. If I suddenly showed up, it would be like two rats in a hole—the most spirited fighter will win." The king approved and Zhao She left the capital at the head of the relief forces. However, he had marched only thirty *li* when he halted the army and began constructing a fortified encampment. For twenty-eight days Zhao She continued to dig trenches and erect stockades. During this time he sent out spies to patrol the countryside. They soon reported seeing a scouting party of Qin troops spying on the encampment. Zhao She ordered that these spies were to be allowed to escape and report back to Qin, and that he be notified the minute they departed.

When the Qin spies reported back that Zhao was constructing a fortified camp the Qin general was relieved, since it meant that they were not going to relieve the siege. He reasoned that since Ouyu was not

---

1. To differentiate this strategy from that of Chapter 6, *Clamor in the East, Attack in the West*, I offer the following quote:

"The essential formula of actual combat is a convergent assault. A commander achieves this by dividing the attacking force into two or more segments. Ideally each segment attacks the same target simultaneously and in close coordination, but from a different direction or approach, thereby holding all enemy elements in the grip of battle and preventing any one from aiding the others. Sometimes one part of a force fixes the enemy in place or distracts him while the other part maneuvers to gain surprise and break up the defense. *A true convergent assault is vastly different from a feint or 'holding attack' by one force with the aim of diverting the enemy from the main blow.*

really inside Zhao territory they were not really concerned about it. The Qin general therefore failed to prepare defenses to his rear concentrating all his forces instead on taking the town. Unknown to the Qin general, Zhao She had broken camp the same day the spies departed and had followed closely behind them arriving on the scene only hours later. The Qin general having relaxed his guard was totally shocked by the sudden appearance of the Zhao forces setting up positions on the favorable North Hill. Caught between the Zhao forces to their rear and the Ouyu garrison in the front, the Qin suffered a serious defeat and were forced to flee across the border.[2]

QIN DYNASTY CHINA

Toward the end of the Qin dynasty there were numerous rebellions as the old kingdoms broke away from central imperial rule. The most powerful of the rebel leaders was Xiang Yu, warlord of western Chu. He proclaimed that any rebel general that succeeded in capturing the Qin capital would be granted the territory of Qin as reward. But when the capital was captured by a mere peasant rebel named Gaozu,[3] Xiang Yu was not pleased since he had fully expected to capture the capital himself. Gaozu, however, wisely refused the honor

---

[Italics mine.] Countless commanders over the centuries have wrecked their hopes with obvious feints that an astute enemy recognized, or they have tried to hit an objective that was so divided or spread out that the enemy was not distracted and could bring up forces to repel each blow."

—Alexander, Bevin, HOW GREAT GENERALS WIN.

I have therefore interpreted strategy No. 6 as the feint and distraction, and strategy No. 8 as a convergent assault.

2. From Du Mu.

3. In Chinese written history emperors are known by several names depending on what point in their career the story takes place. In this instance, the founder of the Han dynasty is called Liu Qi

and was given instead the governorship of the remote province of Han. This in effect exiled Gaozu and spared Xiang Yu both the embarrassment and threat of his presence at court. The shortest path to reach Han was through a precipitous valley where part of the road consisted of a wooden walkway that ran along the steep cliff walls and which was supported by beams inserted into deep holes carved into the solid rock. Gaozu's advisor, Jiang Liang concerned that Xiang Yu might think them too much of a threat to allow them to escape said, "Would it not be wise to burn and destroy the wooden roadway which you have passed over? This would prove to the world that you have no intention of marching east[4] again and thus set Xiang Yu's mind at ease." Gaozu agreed and the army burned the walkway as they passed. However, after a month of preparation, Gaozu was ready to march east and fight Xiang Yu for control of the empire. First he ordered a large work detail to begin repairing the wooden walk-way while secretly sending his main force along narrow mountain trails through Chencang. When news that they were repairing the walkway reached Xiang Yu, he ordered the king of Yong, Chang Han, to lead an army and position themselves at the terminus of the walkway. There they could bottle Gaozu's forces in a narrow valley leaving them with no chance of breaking out. This was the obvious strategy for such a situation and Gaozu had count-

---

while he was still a peasant, the duke of Bei when he became a general, The king of Han when he was assigned the kingdom of that name, Liu Bang when he became emperor (although the use of this name was forbidden during his lifetime and so it never appears in the historical records of his time), and finally his posthumous title, Gaozu. To avoid unnecessary confusion I have used the posthumous title Gaozu throughout, since this is the name most often used in the official histories.

4. "Marching east" refers to the direction of the capital, thus implying an ambition to claim the imperial throne.

ed on whoever was sent to oppose him to use it. Meanwhile Gaozu's general Han Xin, who had set out weeks earlier, came out of the mountains well behind Chang's troops waiting at the valley entrance. They launched a surprise attack from the rear while Gaozu and his troops charged out of the valley from the front. Chang was defeated but managed to escape to the capital with the news. Xiang Yu sent out three armies to attack Gaozu chasing him all the way to Zhongyang where Gaozu and the remnants of the Han army were trapped. Gaozu would triumph in the end but not until after he employed the strategy *Shed Your Skin Like the Golden Cicada* (see Chapter 21).[5]

MUROMACHI PERIOD JAPAN

In 1560 one of Japan's greatest warlords, Oda Nobunaga, then still a minor commander, marched his force of two thousand men to stop the incursion of a rival warlord, Imagawa Yoshimoto. Even though Nobunaga was outnumbered twelve to one he set out humming a tune. Nobunaga's scouts reported that Imagawa was resting his troops at a village that was nestled near a narrow gorge that Nobunaga knew would be ideal for a surprise attack. The scouts further reported that Imagawa's troops were celebrating and viewing the heads taken in a previous battle. Nobunaga devised the following ploy. He made camp some distance away from the village. He placed numerous flags and had straw dummies made to give the impression that a large host had arrived. Imagawa's forces thus expected an attack to come from the direction of the enemy camp. Meanwhile Nobunaga's troops secretly made a forced march in a wide circle in order to come up from behind the Imagawa encampment. Weather favored Nobunaga's

---

5. From RECORDS OF THE GRAND HISTORIAN.

scheme, for late in the day there was a heavy downpour. Taking advantage of the foul weather, Nobunaga's troops launched a sudden attack from the rear. So unexpected was this attack that Imagawa first thought that a brawl had broken out among his own troops. Only when he saw two enemy samurai charging towards him did he realize he was under attack. This realization came too late, and Imagawa was beheaded and his troops scattered. The battle lasted only a few minutes, but it made Oda Nobunaga's reputation and he quickly rose to power, eventually becoming one of Japan's greatest warlords.[6]

SUMMARY

Against a seasoned and wary opponent, feints will prove ineffective. Instead one must make an actual attack to gain his attention. Once his forces are concentrated in defending the obvious attack, you attack from a second direction, thus catching him by surprise.

---

6. From HISTORY OF JAPAN 1334-1615.

CHAPTER NINE

第九計

隔岸觀火

OBSERVE THE FIRE ON THE OPPOSITE

To remain disciplined and calm while waiting for disorder to appear amongst the enemy is the art of self-possession.

—SUN ZI

One day a clam exposed on the river bank opened its shell to take in the sun. A snipe came over to peck at the exposed flesh of the clam, which quickly closed its shell to clamp the bird's beak. "If no rain comes in the next two days, there will be a dead clam," said the snipe. "If you don't get your beak free in the next two days, there will be a dead snipe," replied the clam. Then along came a fisherman who easily caught them both.

—*INTRIGUES OF THE WARRING STATES*

Delay entering the field of battle until all the other players have become exhausted fighting amongst themselves. Then go in full strength and pick up the pieces.[1]

WARRING STATES PERIOD CHINA

Wei was at war with Han who called upon Qi for help. The marquis of Qi summoned his ministers and asked them, "Would it be better for us to go to Han's relief immediately or should we wait?" Some advised an immediate expedition before Han was conquered but one advisor disagreed. "Have you not heard that when two tigers fight one will be killed and the other crippled? Neither the troops of Han nor Wei are yet exhausted and were we to go to Han's rescue we would simply be a substitute victim for Wei's armies and our forces would soon be taking orders from Han. At present Wei is intent on having Han, and when Han is about to perish she will surely send another plea for help. We should therefore make a secret treaty with Han offering our support but delay sending any aid until Wei is seriously weakened." The marquis agreed and gave the envoys secret assurances that he would join their side and sent them back to Han. Believing that Qi was wholly behind them, Han fought five battles and lost each one. Only when Han was about to fall did Qi send in her troops who crushed the weakened Wei forces at Maling. With Wei and Han now both near collapse the marquis of Qi forced both to submit to his sovereignty and become vassals of Qi.[2]

---

1. Another parable that describes the same strategy is "sit on the mountain and watch two tigers fight," and is said to be based on the first story. This strategy is almost identical to Chapter 5, *Loot a Burning House*, in that both require your enemy to be engaged with a third party. In the first case the third party is internal turmoil. In the second, the third party is another enemy.

2. From the ZHAN GUO CE.

THREE KINGDOMS PERIOD CHINA

In the early years of the Three Kingdoms Period the warlord Cao Cao had defeated and killed his rival Yuan Shao in the battle of Guandu. After his death, Yuan's three sons began fighting over the succession. Cao Cao decided to launch another attack, but as soon as he began to mobilize his troops the sons united their forces against him. Then one of his ministers, Guo Jian, said, "When we attacked we provided the three sons a common enemy to unite them. Let us bide our time and allow them to resume fighting amongst themselves. After they have weakened themselves we can attack again." Cao Cao withdrew his army and soon the Yuan brothers renewed their squabbling. The elder brother was angry because his father had named his middle brother as successor. The youngest brother supported the middle brother. Eventually the two younger brothers won out and the eldest brother was killed. During this time Cao Cao had started attacking outlying provinces. By the time the eldest brother was killed, the two remaining brothers feared engaging Cao Cao and instead fled to a distant province in the northeast to seek the aid of a nomadic chief named Gongsun Gang. Some ministers urged Cao Cao to pursue the brothers before they could elicit the help of the barbarians, but Cao Cao ordered his troops to withdraw and assured his minister that Gongsun would soon send him the heads of the two brothers. Shortly thereafter a courier brought the two heads neatly wrapped and boxed. When asked by the confounded ministers for an explanation Cao Cao told them, "If I had attacked the brothers, Gongsun would assume that he would be next to fall under my dominion and his logical choice would be to unite with the brothers against me. But if I provided no threat to

Gongsun then the success of the two brothers would be his next immediate threat. Since I did not present the threat, Gongsun was able to eliminate his next possible threat then and there."[3]

HOJO REGENCY JAPAN

In 1583 the great general Toyotomi Hideyoshi was positioning his forces against Akechi Mitsuhide in what would be the battle of Yamazaki. Shortly after the battle had engaged, Tsetsui Junkeian, an ally of Mitsuhide, arrived on the scene. Impressed by the superior forces of Hideyoshi, he refused to attack but instead ordered his men to line up in battle formation on a hill above the Horagatoge pass where he could watch the battle before deciding which general to side with. Seeing Hideyoshi gaining the advantage he betrayed his ally and sent his troops over to Hideyoshi's side. This incident was never forgotten and henceforth the Japanese equivalent of *Observe the Fire on the Opposite Shore* is known as "to wait at Horagatoge."[4]

SUMMARY

When there are several players each competing with the other to attain the same goal, restrain yourself from being drawn into the fray. While it may seem opportunity is slipping past, wait and watch. Either the goal will reveal itself as not worth fighting for, or you can attain it later with far less effort.

---

3. From ROMANCE OF THE THREE KINGDOMS.
4. From HISTORY OF JAPAN 1334-1615.

CHAPTER TEN

第 十 計

笑 里 藏 刀

HIDE YOUR DAGGER
BEHIND A SMILE

*Speak deferentially, listen respect-
fully, follow his commands, and
accord with him in everything. He
will never imagine you might be in
conflict with him. Our treacherous
measures will then be settled.*

—THE SIX SECRET TEACHINGS OF
THE TAI GONG

Charm and ingratiate yourself to your enemy.
When you have gained his trust, you move
against him in secret.[1]

WARRING STATES PERIOD CHINA

The king of Wei sent a beautiful courtesan to the king
of Chu who took great delight in the new girl. His
queen, Zheng Xiu, knowing how fond the king was of
his new woman, treated the newcomer as a sister sup-
plying her with gifts and treasures and whatever she

---

1. The origin of this expression is thought to stem from a Tang
dynasty poet, Bai Juyi, who wrote about a notorious sycophant by

needed. The king, hearing of this, summoned his queen and said, "A woman serves a man with her beauty and thus jealousy is a part of her very nature. Yet you, knowing how much I am pleased by the new woman, have treated her more kindly than I have myself. These actions are those of a child to her parents or a minister to his ruler. How unexpected it is to find this in a queen to her husband." The queen thus knew that her husband did not suspect her of jealousy. When she next met with the new girl the queen told her, "His majesty is much taken with your beauty but he dislikes the shape of your nose. When next you serve him be sure to cover it with your hand." Grateful for the advice, when she next served the king this is what she did.

The next day the king asked his queen, "The new woman covers her nose when she is with me. Do you know why?"

"I know," replied the queen.

"Well then no matter how unpleasant, you must tell me the reason."

"It seems she does not like the way your majesty smells."

"The shrew!" cried the king.

In a rage the king ordered that the unfortunate girl's nose be cut off.[2]

---

the name of Li Yifu who "...hides a dagger behind his smile and murders people."

Another ancient proverb that refers to the same strategy is known as "thick face black heart" (*Ho Lian, Hei Xin*). This single proverb has spawned several Chinese language books dating from the Ming dynasty to the present. The basic theme is to view life in Machiavellian terms. The "thick face" refers to one's ability to hide your innermost schemes under a facade of benign innocence, the "black heart" is one's true ambitions.

2. From the ZHAN GUO CE.

WARRING STATES PERIOD CHINA

In 342 B.C. General Yang of Qin invaded the state of Wei and laid siege to the city of Wu. The king of Wei, already weakened from a previous battle, was unwilling to face another engagement and asked his counselors for advice. One of his officials, minister Ying, said, "General Yang was originally a native of Wei and in our youth he and I were close friends. I therefore request to be allowed to go personally to appeal to our friendship and try to persuade him into lifting the siege." The king agreed and sent the minister to Wu. When he arrived, minister Ying sent a message asking for a meeting outside the city walls in three days to discuss a mutual retreat. When general Yang received the message that his old friend was in charge of the city's defense and was requesting peace negotiations he readily agreed. Three days later minister Ying left the city and, to show his good faith, was accompanied by only three hundred men. General Yang greeted his old friend with open arms and invited him and his men to a banquet. During the celebrations, minister Ying and his men were seized and their uniforms taken. Dressed like Wei soldiers, the men of Qin marched back to the city and ordered the gates opened. As soon as the gates were open they rushed in and seized the city. The trusting minister Ying was taken back to Qin as captive.[3]

YUAN DYNASTY CHINA

In 1320, after the death of emperor Renzong (the great-grandson of Kubalai Khan), there followed two years of turmoil in the court over who should succeed to the throne. One faction installed the nine-year-old son of the late emperor, but the new prime minister, seeing an

---

3. From the ZHAN GUO CE. The Jin general's name was Gongsun Yang (later known as Lord Shang), the Wei minister's name was Gongzi Ying. I found the similarity between the two surnames confusing, so I substituted them with General Yang and Minister Ying.

opportunity to advance his status, conspired to have the young emperor and his supporters massacred. He then sent for Prince Huai, who had been banished to the south years earlier, and installed him on the throne in hopes of manipulating the inexperienced ruler. Prince Huai, however, wanted to make his elder brother Heshi emperor. When Prince Heshi received the message that his brother had become emperor and wanted to hand the throne to him, he became suspicious and refused to go to the capital.[4] In order to assuage his elder brother's fears, the young emperor offered to meet him halfway. Prince Heshi agreed and set out along the road to the capital. When the two brothers met along the road they rushed to clasp each others arms with tears in their eyes. For three days they feasted and drank well into the night. On the morning of the fourth day the elder brother, Heshi, emerged alone from his brother's tent. The body of the emperor was discovered minutes later and Heshi became the new emperor. No one ever mentioned the late emperor or his sudden death again.[5]

SUMMARY

In any contest where the stakes are high, kindness and goodwill are quickly discarded. To hide sinister intentions behind the facade of friendship and loyalty is standard practice in the upper echelons of power.

---

4. Given the history of imperial intrigues, such an offer could not do anything but arouse suspicion.

5. From IMPERIAL HISTORY OF CHINA.

CHAPTER ELEVEN

第十一計

李代桃僵

SACRIFICE THE PLUM TREE IN PLACE OF THE PEACH

Know contentment, and you will suffer no disgrace. Know when to stop, and you will meet with no danger. You can then endure.

—LAO ZI

There are circumstances in which you must sacrifice short term objectives in order to gain the long term goal. This is the scapegoat strategy whereby someone else suffers the consequences so that the rest do not.[1]

---

1. This is an idiom taken from the last lines of a Han dynasty folk song: *"Now, a peach tree grows by a well, and next to it, a plum tree. When worms come to gnaw at the roots of the peach tree, the plum tree instead offers the worms its own roots, and eventually dies. If trees know how to sacrifice for others, it is no surprise that brothers should cast aside brotherly feelings."* From YUEFU SHIJI (A COLLECTION OF FOLK SONGS AND BALLADS).

WARRING STATES PERIOD CHINA

Sun Zi's worthiest opponent was Fan Li, a general of the state of Yue. Against Sun Zi's advice, King Helu of Wu took the army personally to attack Yue. Fan Li, though outnumbered, was confident of winning, since the king's military abilities were not in the same league as Sun Zi's. Fan Li prepared a shock tactic by scouring the kingdom's dungeons and prisons for condemned criminals. He offered the convicts a last chance to earn honor in this world and provide benefits for their families. Since they were to die anyway, if they sacrificed their lives on the battlefield instead, then their names would be restored to honor and their families richly rewarded. With nothing to lose, the convicts agreed. When the two armies met and were arranged into battle formations Fan Li gave the signal for the convicts to play their part. Dressed in Yue uniforms they marched to the front of the lines, drew their swords, and, before the horrified Wu army, cut their own throats before dropping dead to the ground. Taking advantage of the shock and demoralization of the Wu army, Fan Li quickly sent a readied detachment to attack Wu's flanks and in the resulting confusion defeated the Wu army.[2]

WARRING STATES PERIOD CHINA

While in residence at the Qi court, lord Meng Zhang sent his retainer Feng Xuan to collect the taxes from his little fief in Xue. Before he left, Feng asked Lord Meng, "Is there anything I may buy for you when I return?"

"If you see something my house lacks, buy it," replied the lord.

Feng Xuan went to Xue and sent out officers to summon the people to settle their debts. When he had collected all the tallies Feng feigned that he had received

---

2. From RECORDS OF THE GRAND HISTORIAN.

an order from Lord Meng absolving all outstanding debts. He returned all the money, burned the tallies, and returned to Qi. The next day Feng called on Lord Meng who was surprised to see him return so soon. "Why to you return so speedily? Have the debts been collected?" asked Lord Meng.

"They have already been collected," was the reply.

"What did you purchase on your return?"

"My Lord asked me to see if there was anything your house lacked. It was my humble opinion that your castle was filled with precious objects, that your stables abounded with steeds, and the lower palaces with beauties. It seemed that only one thing was lacking, and that was fealty. This I bought my Lord."

"How can one buy fealty?" asked Lord Meng.

"At the moment you hold the little fief of Xue, yet you do not cherish the people there as your own children, but look on them as a source of profit," replied Feng. "Your servant took it upon himself to feign an order from you relieving the people of their debts and they cheered your name. That is how your servant purchased fealty."

Lord Meng was displeased but said, "So be it! You may now rest, sir."

A year later the old king of Qi died and the new king distrusted all of his predecessor's advisors. Lord Meng was informed he was being relieved of his duties and sent back to govern his own fief. Lord Meng and his entourage set out to return to Xue, but when they were still a hundred *li* from the city, all its people, even the elderly and children, came out midway to welcome their lord in joyous celebration. Lord Meng turned to Feng and said, "Your purchase of fealty on my behalf, sir, is apparent to me today."

"My lord," replied Feng, "even the wiliest rabbit

needs more than one bolt hole to escape to in order to survive."[3]

THREE KINGDOMS PERIOD CHINA

On one of his campaigns Cao Cao was running short of food. He asked his supply sergeant what he could do. The sergeant suggested reducing the rations by secretly using a smaller cup to parcel out the rice. Cao Cao praised the sergeant and gave his consent to use the smaller measuring cup. After a few days the soldiers began to complain and accused their commander of cheating them. Cao Cao again called in the supply sergeant and told him the situation.

"I will do anything I can to help, but what would you have me do?" asked the sergeant.

"I'm afraid I am going to have to borrow your head," replied Cao Cao and he had the sergeant decapitated and his head stuck on a tall pole with a banner that read "Caught cheating on supplies by using a smaller measuring cup."[4]

SUMMARY

In order to gain one thing it is often necessary to lose another. Trying to hold on to everything at once may cause you in the end to lose everything. Instead sacrifice smaller concerns to strengthen your more important endeavor.

---

3. From the ZHAN GUO CE. Actually, Feng says in the end that a rabbit needs at least three bolt holes, and he then goes on to bribe and trick both the new king of Qi and the neighboring king of Liang (Greater Wei) into offering Lord Meng a high position at their courts.

4. This story appears in the commentary section of the "Biography of Wei Wudi," HISTORY OF THE THREE KINGDOMS, written by Chen Shou in the Third Century.

CHAPTER TWELVE

第十二計

順手牽羊

SEIZE THE OPPORTUNITY TO LEAD A SHEEP AWAY

While following the rules of strategy and tactics be prepared to take advantage of circumstances not covered by conventional thinking. If opportunities present themselves, then the leader should be flexible in his plans and adapt to the new circumstances.

—SUN ZI

While carrying out your plans be flexible enough to take advantage of any opportunity that presents itself, however small, and avail yourself of any profit, however slight.[1]

A Chinese language edition traces the origin of this strategy to a folk tale that describes a destitute traveler walking along the road when he comes upon a flock of sheep. Making his way through them, the traveler emerges from their midst with a lamb under one arm. He behaves so calmly and naturally that the shepherd never notices him abscond with the lamb. The drifter suddenly finds himself in the middle of an opportunity for dinner and takes advantage of it without breaking stride. This proverb is not really a strategy, since it is

SPRING AND AUTUMN PERIOD CHINA

In 770 B.C. The duke of Chen joined forces with Liu and Qi and together they attacked Song. Since the main body of the Chen army was on campaign, the duke of Song used the strategy *Attack Wei to Rescue Zhao* and attacked the now poorly defended state of Chen. This caused the duke of Chen to break off his invasion of Song and return to rescue his own capital. When the duke of Song heard that the Chen army was returning, he withdrew his army. As the Song army retreated they passed through the small kingdom of Tai who had remained neutral during the war between Chen and Song. An advisor to the duke of Song suggested that since the king of Tai had refused to ally himself against Chen, why not lay siege to the city and take their territory since they were already there. The duke agreed and he ordered his troops to surround the capital of Tai. The king of Tai was outnumbered so he sent a secret message to the duke of Chen asking for reinforcements. A couple of days later the Song scouts reported that the Chen army was approaching. Once again the duke of Song abandoned the field and fled back to his home territory. The siege lifted, the king of Tai threw open the gates and welcomed his new allies into the city. The duke of Chen, finding himself and his troops inside the walls of a foreign city, saw an opportunity that occurs but seldom. He seized the king and made him prisoner while his troops quickly overcame the unsuspecting Tai guards and took control of the city. Duke Chen, with scarcely any fighting, was able to annex another kingdom to his rule.[2]

---

dependent on fortuitous circumstance which you cannot apply at will. Instead, this proverb advises one to always remain alert to the current situation and search for unexpected opportunities.

2. From the ZUO ZHUAN, Legge edition.

QIN DYNASTY CHINA

In 209 B.C. China revolted against years of oppressive Qin rule. The Qin general, Chang Han, was sent out to put down the rebellion. He defeated the forces of Chu and then crossed the Yellow River to lay siege to the city of Chulu in Zhao. The King of Chu gathered his remaining divisions and placed them under the command of General Song Yi. As second in command he appointed the aristocrat general Xiang Yu and sent them to lead the army to rescue Zhao. Song Yi marched the army out but stopped half-way and made camp, where they sat and waited for forty-six days. Xiang Yu was becoming impatient and went to see Song Yi and said, "News has come that the Qin army has besieged the king of Zhao at Chulu. If we lead our troops across the Yellow River at once, we can attack them with our forces from the outside, Zhao will respond by attacking from the city, and we are sure to defeat the Qin army."

"Not so," replied Song Yi. "He who merely slaps at the gadfly on the cow's back will never succeed in killing the pesky lice.[3] Qin is attacking Zhao. If she is victorious in battle, then her troops will be exhausted and we can take advantage of her weakness. If she fails, then victory has already been assured. Therefore it is better to let Qin and Zhao fight it out. You see, when it comes to fighting with a sword, I may not be a match for you,[4] but when it comes to laying out strategy, you are no match for me!" After this meeting there was no love lost between the two generals and Song Yi secretly let it be known that he would reward anyone who assassinated Xiang Yu.

---

3. The implication being that the Qin forces were so numerous that to attack them one by one in the field was like swatting at flies— you would never catch them all.

4. Xiang Yu was a renowned swordsman, while Song Yi was an administrator.

Shortly afterwards Song Yi received orders from the king of Chu to send his son back to Qi to become prime minister. Delighted by his son's promotion, Song Yi and the entire army escorted him back to the capital marching for a whole day until arriving at Wuyan city. That night, and well into the next day, Song Yi and his son celebrated at a drinking party in the comfort of the city while the remainder of the army bivouacked outside. The day was cold and a heavy rain was falling so that the soldiers were chilled and starving. Xiang Yu had had enough and declared before the senior officers, "We joined forces for the purpose of attacking Qin, but instead we have sat here all this time without advancing. The year is lean, the people poor, and our men eat nothing but taro root and pulse. We have no provisions for our army, and yet Song Yi holds a great drinking party. He will not lead us across the river so that we may live off the food of Zhao and attack Qin. Now if Qin should succeed in defeating the newly formed Zhao she will be stronger than before, then what sort of weakness will there be that we can take advantage of? Our troops suffered only a single defeat, yet we are all brought together under Song Yi's sole command so that the entire safety of our state depends on this one move. Song Yi takes no thought for our soldiers, but attends only to his personal affairs. He is a traitor to the altars of our soil!"

Early the next morning Xiang Yu went to make his daily report to the supreme general. When he entered the tent, he quickly drew his sword and cut off Song Yi's head. Then he went outside and announced, "Song Yi was plotting with Qin against Chu. The king of Chu secretly sent me an order to execute him." All the other commanders submitted to him in fear. Xiang Yu became Supreme General and marched his army across the river, and in nine battles defeated the Qin forces. Xiang Yu went on to conquer more than half of the empire before losing to Gaozu, the founder of the Han dynasty.[5]

YUAN DYNASTY CHINA

During the final days of the Yuan dynasty, rebellion had broken out throughout the empire. Initially there were several contenders vying to be the first to found a new dynasty on the imminent fall of the house of Yuan, but the field was narrowed to two: Chu Yuanchang and Chen Yifu. The two armies met at Poyang Lake where a naval engagement was to take place. General Chen had the advantage of both troops and ships. His ships were large and sturdy and he had them lined up side by side across the entire expanse of the lake. He furthermore had the ships joined together with iron chains so as to create an impenetrable barrier. General Chu sent his ships to attack but they were defeated, having failed to break through the cordon. Fortunately for Chu, the next day a violent northwest gale began to blow. Since Chen's flotilla was situated downwind, Chu took advantage of the situation to launch fireboats against the barrier. Soon Chen's troops were in a frenzy to save their ships from both the rising storm and the fire which was fanned into a blazing fierceness by the wind. Taking advantage of the panic and confusion that ensued, Chu launched his own fleet into the attack and they completely defeated Chen's forces. General Chen was killed by an arrow through his eye while general Chu became the founder of the Ming dynasty.[6]

---

5. From RECORDS OF THE GRAND HISTORIAN.

6. From IMPERIAL HISTORY OF CHINA.

SUMMARY

Even the wisest planner cannot calculate certainty into his schemes. The element of chance is ever present and a watchful eye is needed to spot when the door of opportunity is opening.

CHAPTER THIRTEEN

第十三計

打草驚蛇

BEAT THE GRASS TO STARTLE THE SNAKE

Agitate him and ascertain the pattern of his movements. Determine his disposition and so ascertain the field of battle. Probe him and learn where his strength is abundant and where deficient.

—SUN ZI

When no matter what you do you are unable to determine the enemy's situation, pretend that you are going to attack fiercely, and you will learn the enemy's plan. When you know the enemy's plan, it will be easy to gain victory.

—MIYAMOTO MUSASHI

When you cannot detect the opponent's plans launch a direct, but brief, attack and observe your opponent's reactions. His behavior will reveal his strategy.

SONG DYNASTY CHINA

One day, in the county of Jianzhou, there was a man who lost a precious object. The local magistrate, Chen Shuku, was called in to investigate. He questioned several people, but no one could tell him who the thief was. So, Magistrate Chen laid a trap for those he suspected. "I know of a temple," he told them, "whose bell has great spiritual power that can tell a thief from an honest man. Since my investigation is at a standstill we must employ the supernatural powers of the bell to solve the matter." The magistrate had the bell brought to the courthouse and displayed in the rear chamber. Then he had the suspects brought in to testify to their guilt or innocence. He explained to them that if an innocent man touched the bell it would remain silent, but if a guilty man touched the bell it would ring out. After lighting incense and chanting prayers, the magistrate had curtains erected around the bell. Previously he had instructed one of his assistants to secretly smear ink on the bell after the curtains were closed. Each suspect was then told to place his hand through the curtain and touch the bell. As they withdrew their hands Chen would examine them. Everyone's hands were stained except those of one man, who confessed to the theft. He did not touch the bell for fear it would ring.[1]

QIN DYNASTY

The notorious eunuch Zhao Gao is credited with helping to bring down the house of Qin, ending China's first and shortest imperial dynasty. After the first emperor died Zhao Gao conspired with the chief minister Li Si to dispose of the legitimate heir to the throne and install a weak and corrupt puppet emperor, Huhei (see Chapter 14). Having established his influence over the

---

1. From CHINESE TALES & FANTASIES.

young emperor, Zhao Gao was nervous about possible opposition from the other ministers of state. So he devised a test to see which ones would be faithful to him. One day he brought a stag into the court and presented it to the emperor explaining that it was a horse.

"You're mistaken, Prime Minister," said the emperor."You've called a stag a horse."

Zhao Gao turned to the other ministers present and asked them whether it was a horse or a stag. Some kept silent. Others, in an attempt to ingratiate themselves with the true power behind the throne, agreed it was a horse. And still others said it was a stag. The emperor was under Zhao Gao's control to such a degree that he believed he was going insane and that the stag really was a horse. Meanwhile, one of Zhao Gao's spies was recording the answers given by each of the ministers. Afterwards, Zhao Gao secretly framed charges against all those who had said it was a stag and had them executed.[2]

MOMOYAMA PERIOD JAPAN

After almost two centuries of civil war Japan was brought under the military control of one man, Toyotomi Hideyoshi, but he died eight years later leaving a five year-old heir. The Daimyo[3] who had served under Hideyoshi split into two camps: those who supported the heir led by Ishida Mitsunari, and those who secretly supported Tokugawa Ieyasu. For two years tensions between the two camps increased as the remaining Daimyo chose which side to support in the inevitable showdown. In 1600 the two camps met near the small village of Sekigahara and fought what has come to be

2. From RECORDS OF THE GRAND HISTORIAN. For the name of the young emperor, I have used Huhei instead of his reign title, Ershi.

3. The rough equivalent of a feudal baron or warlord.

known as the last great samurai battle. Those supporting Ishida and the heir apparent numbered eighty thousand, while the Tokugawa army numbered seventy-five thousand. The two armies formed battle lines among the rolling hills with neither side having the advantage of terrain. However, positioned on some hills overlooking the flanks of both armies were troops led by Kobayakawa Hideaki, an ally of Ishida. Hideaki's position was a serious threat to the Tokugawa left flank. Yet when the battle began, the Tokugawa forces did not attack them, nor did Hideaki charge down on the Tokugawa. As the battle raged on neither side appeared to be gaining the upper hand so Ishida signaled Hideaki to make his attack, but no attack came. Ishida then signaled frantically and sent messengers urging Hideaki to attack but he still refused to move. Tokugawa was also concerned about Hideaki's refusal to enter the fray since he had secretly agreed to betray Ishida during the heat of battle. It became apparent to Tokugawa that Hideaki was going to use the strategy *Waiting at Horagatoge* (see Chapter 9) and join in with the winning team after the battle was won. Tokugawa ordered a detachment of harquebusiers to charge up the hill and fire on Hideaki's troops. This forced Hideaki into action since he could no longer sit passively observing. He honored his secret agreement with Tokugawa and charged down on the flank of his former ally Ishida. Hideaki's defection helped turn the tide of battle. The Tokugawa forces prevailed and Ieyasu went on to become Shogun and found the Tokugawa dynasty.[4]

4. From THE SAMURAI.

SUMMARY

A seasoned warrior knows this strategy well and will not reveal his true intentions. But the inexperienced, nervous of making a mistake in such a high stakes game, will overreact to feints and will thus reveal their weakness.

CHAPTER FOURTEEN

第十四計

借尸還魂

BORROW A CORPSE
TO RAISE THE SPIRIT

In the spirit religion there is what is called the mystery of the spirits. The mystery is kept secret to foster religious faith. When people have faith, they and others benefit from it. In the Warrior's Way, this is called strategy. Although the strategy is falsehood, when the falsehood is used in order to win without hurting people, the falsehood becomes true.

—YAGYU MUNENORI,
FAMILY BOOK ON THE ART OF WAR

Take an institution, a technology, or a method that has been forgotten or discarded and appropriate it for your own purpose. Revive something from the past by giving it a new purpose or to reinterpret and bring to life old ideas, customs, and traditions.[1]

---

1. The origin of this proverb lies in the mystic sects of Taoism. Here the expression is used literally in the manner of spirit possession. The medium, lends his "corpse" so that the spirits of the dead

QIN DYNASTY CHINA

In 212 B.C. the first emperor of China, Qin Shihuangdi, died while touring his empire. The emperor had always been afraid of death and was constantly ingesting various "immortal elixirs" provided by a host of mystic frauds and pretenders.[2] To suggest that the emperor would one day die implied that he was a fool for taking these potions, which was tantamount to treason. No one dared mention the possibility of his mortality to him and as a result he left no instructions as to who should succeed him. There were only two others present when he died: the chief minister Li Si, and the eunuch Zhao Gao. They plotted to keep his death a secret until they could decide for themselves who to place on the throne. While the emperor's eldest son Fushu was the natural choice, both men dreaded his accession as it would mean their fall from power. To rid themselves of this potential threat they sent an order signed with the name of the emperor demanding that Fushu and his loyal general, Meng Tian, both commit suicide. The general suspected a plot and told the prince that he had three hundred thousand soldiers under his command and that they should march on the capital and demand an explanation from the emperor. But Fushu was so deathly afraid of his father, who was infamous for his harshness and cruelty, that he dared not

---

can speak through him. In the history of China's dynastic disputes this strategy involved supporting a pretender to the throne, or if no legitimate heir exists, creating one, such as the long lost descended of a previous dynasty. In the Hong Society there is a legend that the five founders of the order were joined in their struggle against the Qing dynasty by a youth who mysteriously appears and claims to be the last living descendant of the Ming dynasty bloodline. This was an obvious invention to give the organization a "legitimate" pedigree. A similar use of this strategy can be seen today in the buying of English titles. For a princely sum, commoners can purchase the rights to being called duke or marquis.

2. Many of these potions were known to contain strychnine and mercury and some historians believe that the emperor may have slowly poisoned himself to death.

question the imperial order lest some punishment even worse than death be visited upon him. Without further inquiry he committed suicide and his loyal general soon followed suit. Fushu's younger brother Huhei, who had been in on the plot to eliminate his brother, was installed on the throne under the control of Li Si and Zhao Gao. The young emperor was kept busy in the imperial harem while the two cronies took control of the government (see Chapter 13). They were so corrupt and inept that shortly thereafter the entire empire was in open revolt. Within two years all three had been executed and the House of Qin disappeared from history.[3]

HAN DYNASTY CHINA

When the emperor Huidi died in 188 B.C. he left no heir. His mother, the empress Lu, bought a child several years before his death and had her daughter-in-law pretend that it was her own. To cover her tracks the empress had the boy's natural mother executed. After the emperor's death, the empress had this boy installed on the throne with herself as regent. However, within two years the boy, after learning that his true mother had been executed, was heard to say, "When I become emperor I will know what to do." When the empress's spies reported the words spoken by the young emperor she had him murdered and another puppet set in his place. The empress ruled a prosperous empire for eight years through the six successive child emperors that she installed on the throne before dying of a mysterious illness. Rumor said her death was the result of a curse from one of her late husband's concubines, who was horribly mutilated and tortured according to the empress's precise instructions.[4] The empress Lu is remembered in

---

3. From IMPERIAL HISTORY OF CHINA.

4. So horrible was the punishment meted out by the empress that her true son and heir, when shown the results of her handiwork, went insane, and died a year later.

Chinese history as one of three notorious "dragon ladies" who had seized the imperial throne.[5]

THREE KINGDOMS PERIOD CHINA

During the last stages of the crumbling Han dynasty the country was split apart by four warlord generals who had rebelled against the throne, each one seeking to found his own dynasty. The last Han emperor, Xiandi, was captured while on campaign against one of the four generals, but he managed to escape with a small entourage and make his way back to the war-torn capital of Luoyang. The confused and frightened emperor was planning to hide in a ruined palace until the trouble blew over, but was discovered by spies working for another warlord named Cao Cao, who hurriedly marched his army to the desolate capital and captured the emperor. Cao Cao offered the emperor his "protection" which the emperor could hardly refuse. Thereafter the emperor was kept under close guard and used only to sign proclamations drawn up by Cao Cao who thereby claimed to be acting on behalf of the Han Dynasty's true emperor. For twenty years the emperor was used as a puppet behind which Cao Cao ruled until the emperor retired and handed over the seals of government. Cao Cao thereupon founded the short lived Cao Wei dynasty. To prevent any future resurrection of the Han Dynasty, Cao Cao had the retired emperor and all remaining relatives assassinated, thus bringing an end to the great Han dynasty.[6]

---

5. From HISTORY OF THE FORMER HAN DYNASTY.

6. From ROMANCE OF THE THREE KINGDOMS.

HEIAN PERIOD JAPAN

In the 11th century the warrior monks known as *Yamabushi* formed large monastic communities in the mountains surrounding the capital of Kyoto. Over time their ranks increased and their power grew to the point that each monastery maintained a private army. From time to time these monk armies would march into the capital to demand favors and concessions from the emperor, who by this time had become merely a figure-head. Although feared for their fighting prowess with a *naginata*,[7] the monks also employed another tactic in the form of psychological warfare. They would carry into battle a huge portable shrine, known as a *mikoshi*. Within the shrine it was believed there lived the spirit of one of the many gods the Yamabushi worshipped. Any offense against the *mikoshi* was considered an offense against the deity itself. During battle, enemy archers dared not unleash their arrows into the Yamabushi ranks for fear of striking the *mikoshi* and incurring the wrath of god. At other times the monks would carry the mikoshi into the town square, chant curses on the townsfolk and return to the mountains leaving the mikoshi in the village. The towns people were loath to go near it believing the town and everyone in it was cursed by its presence. Only after the townsfolk had gathered together a suit-able "donation" would the monks return and haul the dreaded shrine away.[8]

---

7. A halberd type weapon with a long curved blade at the end of a pole.

8. From HISTORY OF JAPAN 1334-1615.

SUMMARY

Symbols, myths, institutions, and philosophies have an inherent moral and emotional power. This power can be appropriated and used to serve the goals of a higher-strategy.

第十五計

調虎離山

LURE THE TIGER DOWN THE MOUNTAIN

With regard to heights, if you occupy them before the enemy you can wait for the enemy to climb up. But if he has occupied them before you, do not follow but retreat and try to entice him out.

—Sun Zi

Never directly attack a well entrenched opponent. Instead lure him away from his stronghold and separate him from his source of strength.[1]

---

1. To distinguish between a true retreat and an attempt to lure one from his position, Sima Yi offers the following observation:

Whenever soldiers retreat with their flags confused and disordered, the sounds of the large and small drums not

THREE KINGDOMS PERIOD CHINA

In the year A.D.199 Sun Ce had consolidated his newly conquered territories in the south and his next goal was the prosperous area of Lujiang to the north. However, Lujiang had a professional army and was well defended. In addition it also had the advantage of terrain, being accessible only through a couple of easily defended passes. Sun Ce's advisors cautioned against moving directly against such a well entrenched and powerful state so they devised another scheme. Sun Ce sent an emissary laden with gifts and a letter to the king of Lujiang, Liu Xun. The letter praised the king's military skills and begged for his assistance. Sun Ce wrote, "For

---

responding to each other, and their orders shouted out in a clamor, this is true defeat, not unorthodox strategy. If the flags are ordered, the drums respond to each other, and the commands and orders seem unified, then even though they may be retreating and running, it is not a defeat, and must be a case of unorthodox strategy. THE ART OF WAR says "Do not pursue feigned retreats."

—SEVEN MILITARY CLASSICS

This strategy is one of the most basic, yet important lessons of conflict, succinctly summed up as follows:

From the beginning of organized warfare, frontal attacks against prepared defenses have usually failed, a fact written large in military history for all generals to see.

—ALEXANDER BEVIN, HOW GREAT GENERALS WIN

This is the first of three proverbs that describe a similar tactic. The others are *Toss Out a Brick to Attract Jade* and *Lure the Enemy onto the Roof, Then Remove the Ladder*. All three describe the basic strategy of setting an ambush, and then using something as bait to lure the enemy into the trap. To differentiate between the three, I divided this strategy into three variations: The first, *Lure the Tiger Down the Mountain*, uses bait to lure an enemy out from his defensive position. The second, *Toss Out a Brick to Attract Jade*, refers to the use of a seemingly precious object, such as riches, supplies, or weapons, to lure the enemy into an ambush. The third, *Lure the Enemy onto the Roof, Then Remove the Ladder*, is based on Sun Zi's Chapter on terrain, whereby the enemy is lured into a swamp, up a mountain, or across a river.

years the state of Shangliao has invaded my territory unhindered and carried away booty, yet we are too weak to launch a retaliatory raid. If Your Majesty would attack Shangliao we would give assistance and you could annex the state for yourself." Flattered and covetous of increasing his domains, The king of Lujiang disregarded the advice of his counselors and attacked the state of Shangliao. Several weeks later, while the king of Lujiang was busy laying siege to Shangliao's capital, Sun Ce attacked the almost undefended Lujiang and easily seized the capital. Without the expected support from Sun Ce, The king of Lujiang failed to take the capital of Shangliao and he returned only to find his own capital already in enemy hands. Sun Ce now had the advantage of the Lujiang terrain and the former king could do nothing but flee with his army.[2]

HAN DYNASTY CHINA

The first Han emperor, Gaozu, wishing to destroy the growing menace of the Xiongnu tribes that had been raiding his northern territories, sent spies to report on their condition. Forewarned, the Xiongnu carefully concealed their able-bodied men and well-fed horses and allowed only old men and emaciated cattle to be seen wandering the countryside. When the spies returned they all recommended an immediate attack on the Xiongnu since it seemed obvious that they were poor and starving. However, one of the councilors, Lou Qing, became suspicious saying, "When two countries go to war they are naturally inclined to make ostentatious displays of strength. Yet our spies see only old men and deprivation. This is surely a deception on the enemy's part to lure us into a trap, and it would be unwise to attack." The emperor however disregarded his advice and

2. Shangliao: another state that shared borders with both Sun Ce's and the King of Lujiang's territories.

as predicted they were trapped in the city of Pingcheng. The emperor and his army barely escaped after employing an unorthodox strategy of their own (see Chapter 31).[3]

YUAN DYNASTY CHINA

Lure the Tiger Down the Mountain was a favorite strategy for the Mongol armies since their superior cavalry was better suited to attacking field troops then laying siege to fortified positions. A special unit of the Mongol cavalry known as the *Mangudai* would charge the enemy's front lines and then, apparently beaten back, they would feign a disorderly retreat. Deceived into believing that they were winning, the opposing army would leave their positions and give chase. Once the pursuers had been drawn out into a a long thin line the Mongols would quickly reorganize into two divisions that would split apart in opposite directions and circle back to attack the center of the line of pursuing soldiers. After destroying the center and separating the enemy's forces they could easily overcome the remaining forces up and down the line.[4]

SUMMARY

It is a rule in warfare to avoid attacking what is hard. When an opponent has the advantage of either terrain, defensive works, or home territory, then he is in a position of strength. Through trickery and deception he must be lured away from his advantageous position. Once out in the open he will expose weaknesses that can then be attacked.

---

3. From the ZHAN GUO CE.

4. From CHANG YU.

CHAPTER SIXTEEN

第十六計

欲擒故縱

To Catch Something, First Let It Go

Do not obstruct an army retreating homeward. If you besiege an army you must leave an outlet. Do not press an exhausted invader.

—Sun Zi

Cornered prey will often mount a final desperate attack. To prevent this you let the enemy believe he still has a chance for freedom. His will to fight is thus dampened by his desire to escape. When in the end the freedom is proven a falsehood the enemy's morale will be defeated and he will surrender without a fight.

SPRING AND AUTUMN PERIOD CHINA

In 506 B.C. an alliance of states headed by Wu overran and defeated the army of Chu. The remaining Chu troops were in retreat. The king of Wu wanted to pursue and destroy the fleeing army but was held back by his younger brother Fu Gai who said, "A cornered beast will fight to the finish, how much more an army of warriors. If they know there's no escape and they must fight to the death, they are bound to overpower us. However, if we allow them to reach and cross the river then, once in their home territory, they will think only of escaping the field." The king followed his brother's advice and allowed the Chu army to cross the river. Once on the other side, the Chu soldiers began preparing food since they had not eaten in a long time. When the Wu army finally arrived on the opposite shore, the Chu soldiers abandoned their cooking fires and scattered into the countryside. The Wu army followed after and easily conquered the Chu capital of Yingdu.[1]

HAN DYNASTY CHINA

The Han general, Zhao Zhongguo, was sent to conduct a campaign to drive out a tribe of Xianling barbarians who had invaded the western provinces. By the time the

---

1. From the ZUO ZHUAN, Watson edition.

general arrived in the area the Xianling had been pillaging for months and were negligent and lax in their guard. They were no longer in the mood to fight and were intent on making off with their booty. When they saw the great Han army approaching from a distance, they panicked, abandoned their baggage train, and withdrew towards the Huang River. Their route of retreat was narrow and constricted, so general Zhao proceeded slowly. Some of his commanders were eager to close in fast on the retreating tribesmen, but Zhao said, "These impoverished invaders can not be hastily pursued. If we proceed slowly they will depart without paying much attention to us; if too quickly, they will turn about and fight to the death." His commanders half-heartily agreed. The Xianling, seeing in the lax pursuit an opportunity to escape unharmed, dashed madly into the Huang River to flee. Several hundred drowned, while the remainder threw down their weapons and scattered into the countryside. Thus without engaging in battle or suffering any casualties, General Zhao succeeded in inflicting heavy casualties and completely routing the enemy.[2]

SIX DYNASTIES PERIOD CHINA

In A.D. 384 a district administrator named Hong allied himself with the local tribes and rose up in arms against the emperor of the Former Qin. The emperor sent General Fu to quell the rebellion. General Fu was renowned as being a fierce commander who showed no pity for either the enemy or his own troops. When the rebel Hong heard that general Fu was leading the army against him he prepared to flee the state. General Fu drove his soldiers fast in order to intercept Hong and prevent him from escaping. One of General Fu's advi-

2. From HISTORY OF THE FORMER HAN DYNASTY.

sors said, "Hong and his tribesman have a mind to go home. It behooves us to allow them to escape beyond the pass rather than obstruct them." But General Fu did not agree with this advice and urged his men on even faster. He finally caught up to Hong and his tribesmen at the Hua Marsh. There Hong and his men were on desperate ground and turned to fight. Because of the entangling terrain, General Fu could not make effective use of his superior numbers, while Hong's tribesmen were determined to fight to the death. The result was that the Qin forces suffered an unexpected defeat and General Fu was killed. Hong went on to carve out his own autonomous kingdom that remained free from imperial rule until his death.[3]

SIX DYNASTIES PERIOD CHINA

During the Southern Song period General Tan Daoji launched an attack against the north on behalf of the emperor. Throughout the campaign he seized cities and destroyed fortifications, taking more than four thousand prisoners. His advisors suggested that he should execute them all and erect a victory mound with the dead. Tan Daoji replied, "At this time we have attacked the guilty and consoled the people. The army of a true king takes the upright as its position, so why is it necessary to slay the people?" He released all the prisoners and sent them back to their homes. These former prisoners told their kinsmen of their capture and release and of the fair treatment they received at the hands of general Tan. Thereupon the barbarians dwelling in the region were elated, and wherever general Tan went a great many came forward to give their allegiance to the emperor.[4]

---

3. From THE CHRONICLES OF FU JIAN.

SUMMARY

Sun Zi wrote that if you place your troops in a desperate situation they will fight for their lives. When the advantage of power lies in your favor you must beware not to place the enemy's forces in a position where they will fight to the end against you. By allowing the possibility of escape you undermine the moral basis for a last ditch battle.

---

4. From IMPERIAL HISTORY OF CHINA. Almost a thousand years earlier, during the Spring and Autumn Period, Duke Suan of Chu invaded and defeated a large army of Jin. His advisors suggested he build a huge victory mound out of the dead soldiers and equipment so that all may know how mighty the Chu armies are. The Duke rebuffed such suggestions by recalling an incident that occurred almost a thousand years before his time during the founding of the Zhou dynasty. After having overthrown the last Shang dynasty, King Wu is counseled to slaughter the population, to which he replies:

He has called in the shields and spears,

He has returned to their cases bows and arrows,

I will seek true virtue, and display it throughout the great land,

That as king I may indeed preserve our appointment.

Thus we have three almost identical situations, each separated by almost a thousand years.

CHAPTER SEVENTEEN

第十三計

打草驚蛇

Toss Out a Brick to Attract Jade

*Bait them with the prospect of gain,
bewilder and mystify them.*
— Sun Zi

Prepare a trap, then lure your enemy into the
trap by using bait. In war the bait is the illusion
of an opportunity for gain. In life the bait is the
illusion of wealth, power, and sex.

WARRING STATES PERIOD CHINA

The earl of Zhi was preparing to attack Lesser Wei. To prepare for his attack he presented the king of Wei with four hundred mustangs and a beautiful white jade *bi*.[1] The king was overjoyed and his ministers all offered their congratulations, but one minister, Nanwen Ci, looked distressed. The king seeing his demeanor asked, "The great state is very pleased with us! Why then do you look troubled?" The minister replied, "One must always examine thoroughly a reward given for no merit and deference shown where no force has been applied. Four hundred mustangs and a white jade *bi* constitute the kind of gift a small state might give when serving a great one. But in this case the larger state makes the gift. Your majesty should ponder this." As a precaution, the king of Wei told his commander of the border guards what his minister had cautioned and ordered his troops to be on full alert. Shortly thereafter, as the minister intimated, the earl of Zhi arrived at the border with a large army. But when the earl saw the border guards posted at full strength, he retired saying, "Alas, there are worthy men in Wei, for they have anticipated my plans."[2]

HAN DYNASTY CHINA

During the Han dynasty, General Li Mu was sent north to deal with the continuing problem of the Xiongnu. Every time General Li sought to fight a decisive battle with the nomads they would melt away into the endless expanse of the grasslands. Seeking to entice them into a

---

1. A ceremonial ornament taking the shape of a carved disc or a carved pillar. These were highly valued in ancient times, though their exact purpose remains a mystery.

2. From the ZHAN GUO CE.

position where they could be attacked, General Li devised the following strategy: He departed southwards with the main body as if returning home, but he ordered that his baggage train and accompanying heard of cattle lag behind. The Xiongnu, believing the general had given up, saw an opportunity to raid his trains and capture the prized herd. They followed behind the retreating army waiting for the right moment to seize the baggage train. Each day General Li allowed the baggage train to trail further behind until he came to a fork in the road that was surrounded by gently rising hills. Judging this terrain to be ideal for his plans, General Li positioned his best troops in ambush behind the hills. He then gave orders for the baggage train to rest in the fork while the remainder of the army continued along the road. The Xiongnu, seeing the main body off in the distance while the baggage train was resting unprotected, rushed into the valley to attack. There they were ambushed from three sides, and over one hundred thousand nomad cavalrymen were killed.[3]

THREE KINGDOMS PERIOD CHINA

General Cao Cao of Wei used a similar tactic in his campaign against his rival, General Yuan Shao. Hearing that Yuan Shao had crossed the Yellow River and captured a vassal city of Yanjing, Cao Cao led an army out against him. As he neared the enemy's territory Cao Cao had his column reverse positions so that the baggage train led while the army took up the rear. He ordered the army to lag further and further behind until the baggage train was over two hours ride ahead of the main army. The baggage train was thus the first to encounter the advancing army of Yuan Shao. The train handlers and guards, upon seeing the approaching army, abandoned

---

3. From Du Mu.

the supplies and ran back down the road to warn Cao Cao of Yuan Shao's approach. Several advisors became anxious at this news but Cao Cao brushed off their concerns and even ordered his men to dismount, abandon their horses, and rest up on the side of a hill overlooking the main road. Soon after Yuan Shao's army slowly came down the road encumbered by the plundered supplies from the baggage train. When the Yuan soldiers saw the abandoned horses they ran about wildly racing to round up as many horses as they could. With the Yuan forces in such total disarray, Cao Cao ordered his infantry to charge down the hill. The Yuan were caught by surprise and could not form battle lines. They were completely routed and the scattered remnants of the army fled back over the border.[4]

SUMMARY

To know where and when your enemy plans to move is to have the advantage of foreknowledge. This can be accomplished by offering your enemy something he greatly desires, then you can control when and where he will be.

---

4. From ROMANCE OF THE THREE KINGDOMS.

CHAPTER EIGHTEEN

第十八計

擒賊擒王

TO CATCH THE BANDITS FIRST CAPTURE THEIR LEADER

Deploy a detachment of shock troops and select commandos to focus their assault on the enemy's vital points.

This is the way to slay their commanders.

—SUN BIN

If the enemy's army is strong but is allied to the commander only by money or threats then, take aim at the leader. If the commander falls the rest of the army will disperse or come over to your side. If, however, they are allied to the leader through loyalty then beware, the army can continue to fight on after his death out of vengeance.[1]

---

1. As a rule, mercenary forces only fight as long as there is someone to sign the paycheck, or if they are in danger of their lives. An enemy who uses mercenary forces is susceptible to assassination, whereas in a national army, where the soldiers and commanders are

SPRING AND AUTUMN PERIOD CHINA

In 756 B.C. the rebel commander Yin Ziqi led an army to lay siege against the strategic city of Suiyang. The defending commander, Zhang Xun, noticed that Yin Ziqi oversaw the siege from well outside the range of the city's archers. He believed that if he could take out the leader the rebel's morale would sink and he would be able to launch a counter attack. He devised a plan with his best archers. The next time the rebels assailed the wall they were to shoot back using the branches of trees. When Yin Ziqi heard that the defenders were reduced to shooting with branches he felt certain the city was ready to be taken. Before the next assault he moved in closer to better oversee the final victory. Riding atop his horse he unknowingly came within range of the archers who had saved their arrows for just such a moment. One arrow hit Yin Ziqi in the left eye killing him instantly. The spectacle of their commander's death in front of almost the entire rebel army served to demoralize them to such an extent that they quickly dispersed from the field.[2]

SIX DYNASTIES PERIOD CHINA

In A.D. 369 there were numerous rebellions against the rule of emperor Fu Jian of the Former Qin dynasty. One rebel general, Li Yan, joined forces with the local hill tribes and proclaimed himself governor of the province of Yi. Fu Jian sent his ablest commander Wang Meng to quell the rebellion. Wang Meng promptly attacked and defeated Li Yan's outlying command posts scattering the tribes back into the hills. Then he chased Li Yan to the city of Fuhan where he laid siege to the city. Li Yan was

related through ancestry, killing the leader would not stop the rest of the army from attacking.

2. From the ZUO ZHUAN.

terrified of being executed and sent his younger brother to seek terms of surrender from the emperor. Wang Meng called out for Li Yan to surrender, but Yan would not come out from behind the city walls. Another commander urged Wang to attack the walls but Wang Meng, refused saying, "I received an imperial order to seize a rebel, not to fight a war." Instead of attacking the walls, Wang Meng employed a Trojan horse strategy. He dressed himself in multi-layered white robes, mounted a ceremonial carriage, and rode up the city gate accompanied by only two unarmed attendants. There he announced that he had come alone and unarmed to personally negotiate a peace treaty with Li Yan himself. Yan, seeing that Wang posed no threat, finally agreed to negotiate and he went to open the gate. Unseen from the city walls, were a handful of armed soldiers, some hidden under Wang's robes, others clinging to the underbelly of the carriage. As soon as Li Yan walked out the gate, these hidden soldiers rushed out and seized the rebel general so fast that his own troops were too dumbfounded to react. They hustled him off in the carriage and Wang Meng returned him to the capital. Without a leader, the province was brought under control without any further battles.[3]

HEIAN PERIOD JAPAN

There was an aristocrat known by the name of Master Yogo who had a dispute over the ownership of some rice paddies with another official named Sawamata. One night, Master Yogo was woken from his sleep to discover that Sawamata had launched a surprise attack. The attackers numbered over six hundred men, and Master Yogo, with less than a hundred retainers, was certain his fate was sealed. Sawamata's troops surround-

---

3. From THE CHRONICLE OF FU JIAN.

ed the compound and set it ablaze with fire arrows. Those who tried to escape the fire were shot down by the archers. By morning all the defenders were dead. Sawamata ordered his troops to bring him the head of Master Yogo but the bodies were so charred they were unable to identify him, although they found his armor on one of the corpses. "In any case, no one escaped alive, not even a dog," said Sawamata. "I am certain that Master Yogo is dead as well." Sawamata and his men left the charred ruins to return home. On the way back they stopped at the mansion of an elderly aristocrat to seek food and fodder as well as medicine for their wounded. Sawamata told his tale to the Great Prince who said, "I'm impressed that you were able to kill Yogo in so brilliant a fashion. He was extremely clever, a man of such ferocity and energy that I wouldn't have expected you could trap him in his house and kill him. Well, now I trust you have his head tied to your saddle and I would like to see it."

"That's a ridiculous request. I told you all that was left were burned corpses. Surely, you wouldn't expect me to carry around such a disgusting thing as a charred head," replied Sawamata.

"Yes, I understand. It's just that from an old man's experience I would feel much more at ease if I knew his head was tied to your saddle just in case it revived. But since it isn't, I cannot take the risk that Yogo is still alive and that I would be caught having to defend someone as unreasonable as you. Therefore you must leave immediately! However, I will send you all the provisions your men need." Sawamata deferred to the elderly prince and he and his troops continued along the road. A short time later several carts carrying the food and fodder arrived and they stopped to unsaddle their horses and heat the wine. After having fought through the night and then marching until late day, Sawamata's troops were near exhaustion. They eagerly drank down the wine and ate the food, after which they all fell asleep along the side of the road. Unbeknownst to Sawamata, Master Yogo was still alive. The night before he had decided fighting was futile, so he dressed a corpse in his armor and, with a handful of men, slipped through the latrine and swam out through a narrow canal to escape. While Sawamata was still at the Great Prince's mansion, Master Yogo had managed to round up some men from the countryside so that they now numbered fifty. A scout reported that Sawamata's troops were all asleep in the fields not far away. Master Yogo turned to his men and said, "Now is the time to strike. Presently they believe me dead and are drowsy from food and drink. If we attack with our fifty men now we may still have a chance." Master Yogo and his men attacked and caught Sawamata's troops by complete surprise. Many fled in panic while others were slain reaching for their saddles and weapons. Sawamata was killed, and Master Yogo made sure to tie his head to his saddle.[4]

SUMMARY

To kill a poisonous snake you must cut off the head. For if you should you cut the snake in half, then the section containing the head may yet coil suddenly and bite. To destroy an opponent you must destroy the command structure to insure that the defeated do not merely find another leader.

---

4. From KONJAKU MONOGATARI (v. 25; sec. 5). Source: LEGENDS OF THE SAMURAI.

第十九計

CHAPTER NINETEEN

釜底抽薪

STEAL THE FIREWOOD FROM UNDER THE POT

When attacking a strong force, it is difficult to attack it directly as it stands. In these cases, one attacks the corners. In large scale battles, after careful inspection of the enemy's forces, one can gain advantage by attacking the corners of exposed strategic points. When one has eliminated the strength of the corners, the strength of the whole will also be diminished.

—MIYAMOTO MUSASHI

When faced with an enemy too powerful to engage directly you must first weaken him by undermining his foundation and attacking his source of power.

— 91 —

WARRING STATES PERIOD CHINA

The king of Wei had amassed and trained a large army with which he intended to expand his territories. The strength of his army frightened several neighboring barons and princes into supporting his dreams of conquest and, with twelve lords pressed into an alliance, he went to the emperor to receive permission to increase his territories.[1] With his imperial blessing in hand the king of Wei first set his sights on Qin. The king of Qin realized his territory would be the first to fall under the Wei expansion and convened his council for advice. One advisor by the name of Wei Yang asked permission to travel to Wei so that he could prevent the army from attacking.

"And how do you plan to accomplish this?" asked the king.

"Have you not heard that defeat can be achieved at a banquet, generals captured while in a sitting room, cities razed between wine and the spiced meat, and a battering ram broken by a sleeping mat." The king confessed he hadn't and gave permission for Wei Yang to travel to Wei and try this unusual strategy. When Wei Yang arrived at the Wei court his reputation enabled him to have an audience with the king. There he said to the king, "Your majesty's accomplishments are great. Your order is obeyed throughout the land, and you are leader of the twelve lords. Soon you will control enough of the country to become emperor. However, to be recognized as emperor you must look and act like an emperor. The first step would be to build a palace befitting an emperor of the realm." The king was flattered and immediately began construction on a massive scale to increase the size of his palaces. Then Wei Yang told the king, "Now you must begin to look like an emperor and wear the scarlet robes,

---

1. This was a mere formality since the Zhou dynasty emperors were by this time reduced to powerless figureheads.

raise the nine pennants of power, and fly the flag of the Red Bird Constellation.[2] The king could not resist flaunting his power openly and he was soon walking about dressed in red robes and accompanied by imperial pennants and flags. It soon became apparent to everyone in the empire that the king of Wei had visions of becoming emperor. This angered the noble houses, especially those of the more powerful kingdoms of Chu and Qi, any one of whom would have a far more legitimate claim to the throne than that provincial upstart, the king of Wei.

Through Wei Yang's subtle manipulations the twelve lords were persuaded to secretly switch their allegiance to Qi. When a large Qi army penetrated the Wei border, the king of Wei called on the twelve lords to stop the invasion. But they captured the king instead and placed him in prison. When the Qi army arrived they installed another prince on the throne of Wei and, to prevent Wei from becoming too powerful in the future, parceled out much of its territory to the neighboring kingdoms. Thus, while the king of Qin sat calmly watching, Wei Yang was able to avert the impending attack by Wei, bring down its king, and annex a portion of Wei territory, without so much as drawing a weapon. After receiving the king's honors Wei Yang said, "This is what is meant by defeat achieved at a banquet, generals captured while in a sitting room, cities razed between wine and the spiced meat, and a battering ram broken by a sleeping mat."[3]

THREE KINGDOMS PERIOD CHINA

The rebel warlord Cao Cao was on campaign against General Yuan Shao when he was joined by a third general, Xu Yu, who inquired about their current situation. Cao Cao replied, "We have only one month of supplies left while General Yuan has a year's worth of provisions stored within easy access at his garrison at Wu Chao. As

2. Regalia that only an emperor could assume.

3. From the ZHAN GUO CE.

it stands now we will be defeated within a month."
General Yu thereupon devised the following stratagem.
He ordered a division of his elite cavalry to dress as
Yuan troops and to muffle their horses hooves by wrap-
ping them in cloth. The disguised cavalry set out the
next night carrying Yuan banners. Whenever they
encountered a real Yuan patrol or checkpoint, the cap-
tain would tell them they were safeguarding Yuan's rear
against a possible sneak attack. Silently arriving at the
garrison by dawn, the elite cavalry took the Yuan troops
by surprise and succeeded in setting fire to the stores.
When the report made its way through the Yuan army
that their provisions had been destroyed, they quickly
surmised that they were now the ones at risk of starvation. The Yuan troops lost their will to fight and three
days later General Yuan Shao was defeated and killed.[4]

LEGENDARY ERA JAPAN

Japan's ancient hero Yamato Takeru was one of the
eighty children of Emperor Keiko. One day he was sent
to kill a notorious outlaw who was such an expert
swordsman that all who had gotten in his way were
killed. Yamato Takeru did not intend to duel with the
bandit and pretended to be ignorant of the man's reputation in order to befriend him. They became such good
friends that they even went swimming together on a
regular basis. When Yamato Takeru was assured the
bandit harbored no suspicions, he was ready to act. One
day when they went swimming he brought with him a
wooden sword that he hid in his travel kit. They were in
the habit of racing each other around a small island, but
this time while they were racing Takeru let the bandit
take the lead. Once he was out of sight behind the

---

4. This story appears in the commentary section of the "Biography
of Wei Wudi," from HISTORY OF THE THREE KINGDOMS.

island Takeru swam back to shore and quickly replaced the bandit's sword with the wooden one. After they had gotten dressed Takeru turned to the bandit and revealed his true purpose. The bandit immediately went for his sword, but the wooden sword had become wedged in the scabbard. While he was struggling to draw the wooden sword, Takeru took the bandit's head off in a single stroke.[5]

SUMMARY

The source of an opponent's strength lies in either wealth, resources, or manpower. If in wealth, cause him to incur expenses, if in resources, disrupt the lines of distribution, if in manpower, sow discord.

---

5. From JAPANESE MYTHOLOGY.

CHAPTER TWENTY

第二十計

渾水摸魚

TROUBLE THE WATER TO CATCH THE FISH

Every day have the vanguard go forth and instigate skirmishes with them in order to psychologically wear them out. Have our older and weaker soldiers drag brushwood to stir up the dust, beat the drums and shout, and move back and forth—some going to the left, some going to the right, never getting any closer than a hundred paces from the enemy. Their general will certainly become fatigued, and their troops will become fearful. In this situation the enemy will not dare to come forward. Then when we come forth with our three armies the enemy will certainly be defeated.

—THE SIX SECRET TEACHINGS OF THE TAI GONG

Before engaging your enemy's forces create confusion to weaken his perception and judgment. Do something unusual, strange, and unexpected as this will arouse the enemy's suspicion and disrupt his thinking. A distracted enemy is thus more vulnerable.

SPRING AND AUTUMN PERIOD CHINA

In 632 B.C. the armies of Jin and Chu faced each other at Chengbu before the battle of the same name. Chu sent an envoy to Jin requesting to fight a chariot duel the next day to which the Jin ruler, Duke Wen, agreed. In the morning Duke Wen climbed to the top of an observation tower and looking down on his camp's preparations said, "Young and old conduct themselves according to ritual. They are fit for use!" He then ordered his troops to cut down trees to be used as part of an unorthodox tactic. While the chariot duel was underway Duke Wen launched a sudden cavalry attack against the Chu right wing causing it to collapse in. At the same time as the right was being pushed into the main body, the Jin troops in the center raised the retreat pennants and began pulling back. As the Jin troops retreated they dragged behind them the trees they had cut down earlier that morning. This raised such a dust cloud that the Chu commanders thought the Jin were fleeing in panic and eagerly gave chase. When the main body of the Chu army was enveloped in the cloud of dust they were unable to see that the Jin forces had split into two divisions and had turned around. The Jin attacked in a classical pincer movement on both of the Chu flanks. The result was a resounding defeat after which the Chu general was ordered to commit suicide. Duke Wen had taken advantage of the distraction provided by the chariot duel to launch both a surprise attack, and a retreat, manipulating the Chu forces into a trap.[1]

---

1. From the ZUO ZHUAN, Watson edition.

WARRING STATES PERIOD CHINA

The three central states of Qi, Wei, and Han made an alliance to attack the northern state of Yan which in turn, sought help from the southern state of Chu. The king of Chu sent his general Xing Yang to rescue Yan. Unable to attack the combined forces concentrated in Yan, Xing Yang used the strategy *Besiege Wei to Rescue Zhao*, and captured the Wei city of Yongqiu. Wei and Qi were concerned that with the enemy holding a fortified position to their rear their lines of communication would be cut, so they set off to recapture the city. There were two roads that led to the city of Yongqiu and it was decided that the Wei forces would occupy the western road while the Qi, the eastern. This was to prevent Xing Yang from escaping. Xing Yang had succeeded in drawing the enemy away from Yan but he now had to extricate himself from a near hopeless situation. He resorted to an unorthodox strategy. Knowing the tenuous nature of any alliance during those ruthless times, Xing Yang ordered the west gate opened. By day he sent riders and carriages up the road towards the Wei camp but once they were out of sight in the woods they would wait for a while, then turn around and return. By night he had men run up and down the same road carrying torches. The Qi observers thought that the daytime activity looked suspiciously like envoys bearing gifts and tribute, while the nighttime activity looked like messengers bearing urgent communications. Believing that Wei had struck a deal with Xing Yang and that both were preparing a sneak attack on them, the Qi army withdrew during the night and returned home. The next day the Wei army learned that Qi had abandoned the field and they were left alone to retake the city. Thinking better of the idea, the Wei army also left the field, allowing Xing Yang to return to Chu after having successfully rescued Yan.[2]

---

2. From the ZHAN GUO CE. (What the Han army was doing all this time is not recorded.)

FIVE DYNASTIES PERIOD CHINA

General Li Suyuan of Jin was sent to relieve the siege of Yuzhou and drive the invading Khitan tribes out of the empire. The Khitans set up defensive positions in advantageous terrain with the intention of using the strategy *Await the Exhausted Enemy at Your Ease.* Their plan was to attack the Jin troops before they had a chance to form battle lines. However, General Li's scouts reported that the Khitans were already waiting in formation, giving away their intentions. Li Suyuan ordered his infantry to hold back while the weak and weary soldiers went ahead dragging brushwood and burning fires as they neared the Khitan formations. This created such a cloud of dust and smoke that the Khitan commander could not see the Jin army and assumed the dust was being kicked up by a large infantry. Seeing an advantage, he ordered his men to break formation and attack what he believed would be an army of Jin troops blinded by the smoke and dust. But as the Khitans attacked, the Jin soldiers dropped their branches and ran off so that the Khitans advanced through the dust cloud surprised to discover no army there. As the disoriented Khitan army turned to escape from the clouds of dust, Li Suyuan ordered his army to charge in from the rear. The result was a rout and slaughter. The siege of Yuzhou was lifted.[3]

---

3. From THE STRUCTURE OF POWER IN NORTH CHINA DURING THE FIVE DYNASTIES. In the first story, the Chu attacked through the dust cloud believing they were pursuing a retreating army and could not see the counter attack. In this story, the Khitans thought the Chinese army would be similarly blinded and not see the attack coming.

SUMMARY

Man and beast alike will spontaneously pay attention to anything unusual within their environment. Magicians, card sharks, pick pockets, and prize fighters rely on this trait to momentarily trap the person's attention elsewhere while they secretly carry out another action.

CHAPTER TWENTY-ONE

第二十一計

金蟬脫殼

Shed Your Skin Like the Golden Cicada

Although it does not mindfully keep guard, in the small mountain fields, the scarecrow does not stand in vain.[1]
—Bukkoku Kokushi

When you are in danger of being defeated, and your only chance is to escape and regroup, then create an illusion. While the enemy's attention is focused on this artifice, secretly remove your men leaving behind only the facade of your presence.

Han Dynasty China

In 204 B.C. the king of Han, Gaozu, after escaping his exile through the use of the strategy *Openly Repair the Walkway, Secretly March to Chencang* (see Chapter 8), suffered several defeats at the hands of his old nemesis, the warlord of Chu, Xiang Yu. Outnumbered and defeated, Gaozu fled with his remaining troops to Zhongyang

---

1. From Bukkoku Kokushi (1256-1316), Source: The Unfettered Mind.

where he fortified the city and prepared to make a counter attack. Xiang Yu, however, laid siege to the city cutting Gaozu's supply lines and avenue of escape. One of Gaozu's commanders, Ji Xin, devised a scheme to escape, he said, "The situation is very grave. I beg you to let me deceive Xiang Yu for you by taking your place as king. In this way you will be able to slip away in secret." Gaozu agreed and, while he prepared his escape, Ji Xin had two thousand women from the city dressed like Han soldiers. Before dawn he had the women march out the front gate and form battle lines. The army of Xiang Yu rushed to formation expecting a final showdown with Han. As the first light of dawn began to break, Ji Xin rode forth in the yellow draped imperial carriage of the king and announced to the Chu army, "The food in the city is exhausted. The king of Han surrenders!" While the army of Chu was celebrating their victory, the king of Han and thirty horsemen slipped quietly out of the city. When Xiang Yu learned of the deception he had General Ji Xin burned to death. The king of Han made good his escape and two years later returned at the head of a new army. This time he was victorious while the defeated Xiang Yu was hunted down. The final scene in Xiang Yu's life is one of the most poignant in China's history. Xiang Yu had fled to the bank of the Yellow River with a Han detachment hot on his heels. He was alone since every one of his commanders were now dead or had turned traitor. There was a ferryman who recognized the great general of Chu and urged him to cross over the river before the Han troops arrived. But Xiang Yu refused saying, "I left with the sons and fathers and husbands of Chu, but to return alone without them, how could I face the people with such shame." Instead he paid the ferryman to take his favorite stallion across and free him on the other side. By this time the Han soldiers had arrived and, spotting an old comrade among the troops, Xiang Yu called out, "I hear there is a reward for my head. Since you were a friend of mine I give you this parting gift!" And with that he drew his sword and cut his throat. The Han soldiers rushed to retrieve his head and in the melee cut him to pieces. His faithful horse jumped off the boat to swim back but was swept away by the currents and drowned. Gaozu went on to found China's longest dynasty, the Han, in 202 B.C.[2]

THREE KINGDOMS PERIOD CHINA

The warlord Cao Cao of Wei was pursuing the fleeing army and population of Shu, led by the Heroes of the Peach Grove,[3] Liu Bei and Zhang Fei. The retreating column came upon the Changpan bridge over the Wei River with the enemy army only hours behind. On the opposite side of the river there was heavy forest. Zhang Fei turned to Liu Bei and said, "This bridge is the only crossing point for miles, and provides us with an advantage. You take the army and people across while I hold off the Wei army to give you as much of a lead as possible." After the Shu army had crossed over, Zhang Fei sent his small group of cavalrymen across the bridge into the forest where they tied branches to their horses tails and rode around in circles. Zhang Fei remained sitting on his charger in the middle of the bridge. When the pursuing army of Wei came upon the sight of Zhang Fei alone on the bridge they stopped. Cao Cao noticed the huge dust cloud in the distance behind the woods and suspected a trap. Zhang Fei roared out a challenge to the Wei army but Cao Cao, now convinced this was a ruse, turned his men around to retreat. Zhang Fei see-

2. From HISTORY OF THE FORMER HAN DYNASTY.

3. So called because they swore the oath of brotherhood in a peach grove. A similar oath is sworn by members of almost every secret brotherhood in China.

ing the Wei army turn about spurred his charger towards the Wei as though to attack them single-handedly. This so unnerved the Wei forces that they made a mad scramble to escape the area convinced a trap was closing around them. This trick bought Liu Bei and Zhang Fei enough time to escape with their men and regroup at Jiangling.[4]

SIX DYNASTIES PERIOD CHINA

In A.D. 431 the Song emperor, Wendi, launched a campaign to win back the province of Henan which was under the control of the kingdom of Wei. The emperor sent his general, Tao Cu, to attack Wei. The Song army fought and won more than thirty engagements, penetrating deep into Wei territory. Now, every commander knows that when an army is deep inside enemy territory his supply lines are the most crucial and vulnerable. Wei took advantage of this weakness to secretly send a detachment of cavalry that succeeded in cutting off the Song supply lines. The Song army was without provisions and in desperate straits. Tao Cu was planning to retreat, but this would leave the army extremely vulnerable to a rout and slaughter. To make matters worse, many of his soldiers, afraid and starving, deserted to the Wei side and divulged to Tao Cu's the plan to retreat. The Wei readied their forces to pursue the Song the instant they broke camp. To avert the impending tragedy, Tao Cu devised a stratagem. During the night he ordered his troops to carry baskets of sand and pile them into great heaps within the compound. The Wei scouts, listening to the night-long commotion, were curious and crept closer to the Song positions in order to see by first light what was happening. Tao Cu then had the piles of sand covered by a thin layer of grain.

---

4. From ROMANCE OF THE THREE KINGDOMS.

The next morning the Wei scouts were shocked to see huge piles of grain that they assumed were smuggled in during the night. When the Wei commander heard this, he suspected that the deserters' reports were a ruse to lure him into a trap, and had them all executed. The Wei canceled their planned attack. Two days later the Song army quietly escaped to their home territory.[5]

HOJO REGENCY JAPAN

In 1331 the emperor Go Daigo rebelled against the Hojo Shogunate which had ruled over a series of puppet emperors. The emperor fled Kyoto with the imperial regalia[6] and took refuge in a mountain monastery. The emperor's loyal commander, Kusunoki Masashige, in order to divert the impending attack away from the emperor, erected a wooden palisade on the side of the mountain. When the Hojo army arrived they saw the poor construction of the defenses and rushed to attack the encampment. Kusunoki's troops, though numbering less than five hundred, had constructed several ingenious defenses such as pitfalls, trenches, and logs suspended along the steep slopes that they could unleash to roll down onto the advancing attackers. After several failed attacks the Hojo troops resolved to blockade the fort and starve the defenders out. Kusunoki had only a few days worth of supplies left, and he knew that his troops would soon be too weak to fight. So he devised a strategy in which he could escape without pursuit. A huge funeral pyre was prepared and covered with the bodies recovered from the battlefield. One volunteer remained behind to light the fire and wait for the Hojo troops. Under cover of darkness, Kusunoki

5. From IMPERIAL HISTORY OF CHINA.

6. Consisting of a mirror, a sword, and jewels. They were akin to the nine imperial tripods of ancient China—emblematic of the right to rule.

and his troops quietly escaped through a hidden trench cut through the stockade. Once they were in the mountain forests their familiarity with the terrain enabled them to disperse into the undergrowth. At the same time the funeral pyre was set ablaze and it burned so brightly that it lit up the sky. Hojo sent scouts to find out the cause of the blaze. When they found the compound undefended, the Hojo troops rushed in only to find a huge funeral pyre with a solitary attendant kneeling before the fire. When he was questioned he told them that Kusunoki and his troops, knowing they would be defeated, committed suicide en mass. As the Hojo could see burning bodies among the embers they believed the story and did not search for any remaining troops. Kusunoki escaped that night and he continued to fight for the imperial house for another seven years. He became known as one of Japan's greatest heroes renowned for his unflinching loyalty to the emperor.[7]

SUMMARY

It is a well known rule of war that troops are extremely vulnerable when retreating. A strong attack against retreating troops usually leads to a rout and slaughter. Whenever you are moving troops, leave behind something that will divert or slow potential pursuers.

---

7. From THE SAMURAI.

第二十二計

CHAPTER TWENTY-TWO

關門捉賊

SHUT THE DOOR TO CATCH THE THIEF

When one fights an opponent and it appears on the surface that he has been defeated, if his fighting spirit has not yet been eradicated in his heart of hearts, he will not acknowledge defeat. In that case, you must quickly change your mental attitude and break the opponent's fighting spirit. You must make him acknowledge defeat from the bottom of his heart. It is essential to make sure of that.

—MIYAMOTO MUSASHI

If you have the chance to completely capture the enemy, then you should do so, thereby bringing the battle or war to a quick and lasting conclusion. To allow your enemy to escape plants the seeds for future conflict. But if they succeed in escaping, be wary of giving chase.

WARRING STATES PERIOD CHINA

In 449 B.C. the state of Wu had invaded the state of Yue and carried off its duke, Guo Jian, holding him prisoner for three years before releasing him back to his kingdom. When he returned, Guo Jian planned his revenge. For seven years he ruled with benevolence and generosity, making a reputation as a wise and virtuous ruler until he felt his loyal subjects were prepared to undergo any hardship for him. He accordingly assembled his forces and attacked Wu, gaining a decisive victory (see Chapter 5). The king of Wu had to flee, but it would only be a matter of time before he was caught. He sent ambassadors to Guo Jian begging for mercy. They reminded him of how the state of Wu had released him to return to his own state. The king of Wu now asked to be granted the same favor. Guo Jian was contemplating granting this appeal when his prime minister Fan Li intervened and said, "When heaven gave the duke of Wu the grand opportunity for gaining power, he did not take advantage of it, and so he is a fugitive today. Should you fail to accept what fortune has now given you, you may be driven from your state, and then all the years of hardships you have borne will have been endured in vain." The duke was swayed by the argument and sent the ambassador back with the message that he would not grant any mercy. When the king of Wu received the message he gave up all hope and committed suicide.[1]

TANG DYNASTY CHINA

One of China's most notorious female rulers was the Empress Wu. After dethroning her son, Emperor Zhongzong, she took over the empire and ruled for twenty-two years. During one of the innumerable court intrigues

1. From IMPERIAL HISTORY OF CHINA.

that took place during her reign she suspected two high and corrupt officials of plotting to usurp her power. Using the strategy *It Takes a Thief to Catch a Thief*, she ordered one of those officials, Lai Junchen, to interrogate the other, Zhou Xing. Seeing an opportunity to escape suspicion while eliminating a rival, Lai invited Zhou for dinner and wine to discuss criminal cases. While pouring wine for his guest Lai asked, "Now with some prisoners they simply refuse to confess to their crime. Do you have any suggestions on how they might be made to cooperate?"

"That's very easy," answered Zhou. "You simply take a large metal vat, fill it with water, and place it over a fire until the water is near boiling. Then order the prisoners to get into the vat. They will confess anything and everything."

"Excellent," said Lai, who then ordered a large vat to be brought in and heated the way Zhou had advised. When the water was near boiling Lai stood up from his table and said, "I have received an imperial order to interrogate you on your involvement in a treasonous plot. Now would you please step into the vat."

Zhou was terrified and immediately dropped to his knees to kowtow. He confessed his involvement, and implicated his co-conspirators. All were executed.[2]

MUROMACHI PERIOD JAPAN

In 1554 Mori Montonari sought to avenge the death of his lord, Suye Harukata, who had been overthrown in a palace coup and forced to commit suicide by another retainer. Mori was greatly outnumbered and so decided a stratagem was needed. He constructed a castle on the small island of Miyajima, situated in the inland sea near Hiroshima Bay. After the castle was completed he spread the story that he was regretting his decision since he now realized how susceptible he was to attack by the Suye forces. When the

2. From JIZHI TONGJIAN, Source: 100 CHINESE IDIOMS AND THEIR STORIES.

story reached Suye Harukata he thought it an excellent suggestion and promptly set off to take the castle. The castle turned out to be poorly defended and Suye took the island without bloodshed. He stationed five hundred troops in the castle and the rest of his thirty thousand troops were bivouacked on the island. Meanwhile Mori Montonari captured the town of Kuatsu, directly across the straight from the island. Harukata's troops were over-confident from their easy capture of the island and they failed to even post guards. Mori counted on the element of surprise and chose a moonless night to launch his attack. He hired local pirates to ferry his troops over and made them agree to immediately return so that neither army had the opportunity to escape. Mori divided his flotilla into two columns: one went to the north of the island to attack the Suye from the rear, while the second column crossed further to the south and then hugged the island's coastline to attack from the front. That night there happened to be a blinding rainstorm which further helped conceal the flotilla's approach. Both divisions attacked at dawn and, as expected, caught the Suye army by surprise. Finding that there were no boats in which to escape (it is presumed that the Mori troops scuttled or burned the ships that carried the Suye troops over), the Suye troops committed suicide by the hundreds. Mori had succeeded in luring his enemy into a position from which there was no escape, and in a single decisive battle completely wiped out his opponent.[3]

SUMMARY

While it is dangerous to corner your opponent into fighting to the death, it is equally dangerous to allow that opponent to escape with a hope of revenge. When you have your enemy cornered, leave a door open until his thoughts turn to escape and freedom, then close the trap and destroy him.

---

3. From HISTORY OF JAPAN, 1334-1615.

CHAPTER TWENTY-THREE

第二十三計

遠交近攻

BEFRIEND A DISTANT ENEMY TO ATTACK ONE NEARBY

Let us proceed with caution, concentrating our strength, and add to it daily by winning over to our side those barons who are vassals of the enemy. Then, when the enemy stands alone, like a tree shorn of its leaves and branches, we will attack and destroy the root.[1]

—TOYOTOMI HIDEYOSHI

It is known that nations that border each other become enemies while nations separated by distance and obstacles make better allies. When you are the strongest in one field, your greatest threat is from the second strongest in your field, not the strongest from another field.

---

1. Quote from HIRED SWORDS, THE RISE OF PRIVATE WARRIOR POWER IN EARLY JAPAN.

SPRING AND AUTUMN PERIOD CHINA

In 628 B.C. the states of Jin and Qin joined forces to attack the state of Zheng. They laid siege to the capital, trapping the king in the city. Vastly outnumbered, the king of Zheng could not hope to win militarily. His prime minister said, "The state is in imminent peril. If you summon your old advisor, Chu Zhiwu, and send him to Qin I'm sure he can convince them to depart." The king agreed and summoned the old advisor to explain his mission. That night Chu was lowered from the walls on a rope and he secretly made his way into the Qin camp. Meeting with the earl of Qin he said, "With Jin and Qin both besieging its capital, Zheng knows that it must perish. If the ruin of Zheng were to be of benefit to you I would not dare to speak to you. But you know what difficulties could arise in trying to maintain such a distant border from your capital. It would be constantly threatened by other states. Of what advantage is it to you to destroy Zheng to benefit your neighbor? His advantage will be your disadvantage. And moreover, previously you helped the duke of Jin to attain his position and he promised you two cities as a reward. But as soon as he was in his own state again he built defenses around the two cities.[2] Surely you can see that he is greedy. If you help him to annex Zheng to his domains, who will be next to lose territory to his insatiable hunger? Furthermore, if you agree to depart, the king of Zheng will give you provisions for your army and gifts for yourself. Surely this is no injury. But I leave it up to you to decide whether to diminish Zheng in order to advantage Jin."

The next morning the Qin army left the field. When the duke of Jin saw them returning he also withdrew and Zheng was spared.[3]

---

2. Previously the duke of Jin had reneged on a promise of two cities in return for Qin's help.

3. From the ZUO ZHUAN.

WARRING STATES PERIOD CHINA

The king of Wei was attacking the capital of Zhao and demanded troops from Song. The ruler of Song secretly sent an envoy to the king of Zhao to say, "The forces of Wei are vigorous and their power is great. Presently they are demanding troops from Song to use against you. My lord is afraid that if he does not comply it will mean the end of his country. But if Wei should attack Zhao and truly harm her my lord could not bear it."

The king of Zhao replied, "What can I do to help you?"

"I shall request from you a border town which we will attack slowly. We will spend many days trying to take the town until the time is right for you to send down your officers and reclaim the place again."

"Excellent!" said the king of Zhao.

The Song forces marched out and laid siege to the border town. The king of Wei was happy and said, "The Song forces are aiding my attack." The king of Zhao was also happy and said, "The Song forces will not go any further."

A few months later Song's troops were retired, the crisis avoided, Wei was grateful, and Zhao suspected nothing.[4]

HAN DYNASTY CHINA

In A.D. 110 the province of Henan had suffered through droughts and floods, the harvests were poor and the people starving. The corrupt government only made matters worse, and soon the whole province was in chaos. Any hope of bringing in outside relief was thwarted by the numerous bands of bandits and robbers that roamed the countryside pillaging and terrorizing the population. A provincial official by the name of Yu

---

4. From the ZHAN GUO CE.

Hu was appointed full powers to try to restore some order to the province. When he arrived at the district capital he issued a notice that he was going to organize a military force and that he was looking for recruits. First he promised a pardon for past crimes and immunity for anyone who joined up. Then he announced that he was looking for men for three classes of troops. The first class of troops were to consist of men who had committed robbery and murder. They would be the commanders and receive the highest salaries. The second class would consist of men who had committed mere thievery. They would receive the next highest salaries. The third class would consist of men who had joined the robber bands simply because they were lazy and wished to avoid real labor. They would be paid the lowest salaries. Within a couple of weeks Yu Hu had over three hundred new recruits. When they had been issued uniforms and weapons he had them paraded before him and said to them, "Your past deeds are now forgiven and you are free from prosecution. But you must still atone for the crimes you have committed against society. To do this you must now go out and hunt down all your past colleagues who have not answered my call." This they did and within a year the fraternity of bandits was extinct and the countryside made safe.[5]

SUMMARY

It is well known that a friend of your enemy becomes your enemy while an enemy of your enemy becomes your friend. Every powerful person, organization, or state will automatically create people, groups, and organizations that stand in opposition to it. To attack any objective, one can enlist the aid of those institutions that are the antithesis of your opponent's.

---

5. From THE IMPERIAL HISTORY OF CHINA.

第二十四計

CHAPTER TWENTY-FOUR

假途伐虢

BORROW THE ROAD TO CONQUER GUO

A samurai in service may be said to borrow his master's authority and also rob him of it. And similarly his lord may lend it to him or let him steal it.[1]

— DAIDOJI YUZAN, BUDO SHOSHINSHU

Borrow the resources of an ally to attack a common enemy. Once the enemy is defeated, use those resources to turn on the ally that lent you them in the first place.

---

1. Quote from HIRED SWORDS, THE RISE OF PRIVATE WARRIOR POWER IN EARLY JAPAN.

This strategy at first seems identical to Chapter 3, *Kill with a Borrowed Sword*, where you use another to do the actual dirty work. However, with *Borrow the Road to conquer Guo,"* you use another's sword, but do the dirty work yourself. Finally, you attack the person from whom you borrowed the sword.

Spring and Autumn Period China

The small states of Yu and Guo bordered the larger state of Jin. Duke Xian of Jin desired to conquer both states. This desire was not unknown to the two smaller states and both had taken steps to defend their borders with Jin. The duke's general, Xun Xi, suggested they make a roundabout attack at Guo through the state of Yu to catch them by surprise. General Xun suggested that since the duke of Yu was a greedy man he could be bribed with gifts of jade and horses in exchange for safe passage through his territory. Duke Xian objected to the idea of giving away so much treasure and asked, "What if the duke of Yu accepts our gifts but refuses us passage?" General Xun replied, "If he doesn't intend to let us through, then he wouldn't accept them, but if he does accept the gifts, and he does let us through, then it will only mean that the treasure is stored temporarily in his storehouse rather than ours."

When the bribe was sent to the duke of Yu one of his ministers, Gong Ziqi, cautioned against accepting them saying, "Yu is to Guo, like lips are to teeth. Our ancestors had a saying: 'If the lips are gone, the teeth will be exposed to cold.' Guo's existence depends on Yu, while Yu's ability to survive hinges on Guo. If we make way for Jin, then the day will see Guo perish in the morning only to be followed by Yu in the evening. Why should we ever let Jin pass?" The duke of Yu, however, refused to listen to this advice. Jin was given safe passage and succeeded in conquering Guo. On their way back they stopped to conquered Yu. After taking the Yu capital and recovering the treasure, General Xun returned the jade and horses to the duke. Duke Xian was pleased and said in good humor, "The jade is untouched but the horses seem to have gained some more teeth!"[2]

---

2. *"With the lips gone the teeth are exposed to cold,"* is another famous idiom spawned by this story. The lesson is that there are situations where

WARRING STATES PERIOD CHINA

King Xiong of Qi was of an ungenerous nature. During his father's rule Qi's ablest general was Tian Dan, who had distinguished himself during the war with Yan. When he was still the heir apparent, Xiong worried that the renowned general would seize the throne for himself after the king's death. But Tian Dan was too loyal to contemplate such a move and when Xiong ascended the throne he served under him as minister. One day while Tian Dan was inspecting the countryside he came upon an old man who had just crossed a river. The water was so cold that the old man had collapsed on the bank, too weak to move. When Tian Dan saw this he dismounted and wrapped his own fur cloak around the old man to warm him. When King Xiong heard this he hated Tian Dan and cried aloud, "Why would Tian Dan do a thing like that if he did not intend to take my kingdom from me?"[3] I must have a plan to use against him now or I will be too late."

He looked about for someone to advise him, but the court was empty. Looking out his balcony the king noticed a bead stringer in the street below and called out to him, "Did you hear what I just said?"

"I did," replied the bead stringer.

"And what do you think I should do about this?" asked the king.

"If I were the king I would use him to make me appear good."

---

people and states are so dependent on each other that if one goes down, they all go down. From LUSHI CHUNQIU (Master Lu's Spring and Autumn Annals).

3. In ancient China any official who acted in an upright and moral manner immediately fell under suspicion, since such behavior was thought to be a first step in achieving power. An important factor in war is to fight in accordance with the "moral law"—similar to the Western notion of "having God on your side." Upright behavior was considered courting the moral law.

"How?"

"You should praise the goodness of Tian Dan and issue a statement saying, 'When we are troubled by famine Dan feeds them; when we grieve that our citizens are cold, Dan gives them the cloak from his back. When we are troubled over our people, Dan is troubled. In gauging his king's intentions, none is the equal of Dan, and I praise him.' In this way Dan's virtue will become the king's virtue."

"Excellent!" said the king and the next day he summoned Tian Dan to court. There the king bowed before Tian Dan praising his virtue and awarding him with honors. Then the king turned to the assembly and said, "If any officer should find the people cold and hungry, then he should receive them and provide warmth and food. In this way you would serve your king."

The next day the king's spies returned with the report that in every village the people were saying, "Tian Dan's love for the people is nothing more than carrying out the orders of the king!"[4]

YUAN DYNASTY CHINA

In 1293 the Great Kahn sent twenty thousand troops to subdue the island of Java under the pretext of avenging the murder and mutilation of a Mongol envoy sent earlier. (A more likely explanation is that the Mongols wished to control the lucrative spice trade in the Moluccas.) Using the strategy *Borrow the Road to Conquer Guo* the Mongols made allies with a rebel Javanese prince and his army. Together they succeeded in destroying the local king. However, once the king was defeated the rebel prince quickly turned on his Mongol allies forcing them off the island. Thus the rebel prince used the Mongol sword to destroy his enemy, and then

---

4. From the ZHAN GUO CE.

he used the tactic of *Exchange the Role of Guest for That of Host* to turn on the Mongols after they had weakened themselves fighting the old king.[5]

SUMMARY

In the struggle for power, alliances are formed only if both parties believe they can profit from each other. These alliances last until one party no longer finds profit in the other. The aid you lend an ally might as easily be used against you. It depends whether your ally should find it more profitable to return the favor, or become your enemy.

5. From THE MONGOL WARLORDS

CHAPTER TWENTY-FIVE

第二十五計

偷梁換柱

REPLACE THE BEAMS WITH ROTTEN TIMBERS

The general is the supporting pillar of the state. If his talents are all-encompassing, the state will invariably be strong. If the supporting pillar is marked by fissures, the state will invariably grow weak.

—SUN ZI

Disrupt the enemy's formations, interfere with their methods of operations, change the rules in which they are used to following, go contrary to their standard training. In this way you remove the supporting pillar, the common link which makes a group of men an effective fighting force.

WARRING STATES PERIOD CHINA

In 259 B.C. Qin invaded Zhao, the two armies confronting each other at Changping. After several skirmishes the Zhao forces dug in and waited behind fortified positions refusing to come out despite daily taunts from the enemy. Knowing it was futile to lure the Zhao out, and that a prolonged stalemate worked in their favor, the Qin general schemed to remove the Zhao general leading the defense. Spies were sent to the Zhao camp to spread the rumor that the one thing Qin feared was that Zhao Kuo, son of the famous general Zhao She, would be put in charge of the army. When reports of this rumor reached the king he relieved the current commander and replaced him with Zhao Kuo. What the king of Zhao did not know was that years earlier when the famous general Zhao She was still alive he had tested his son on the art of war and found him wanting. While the son proved knowledgeable in all aspects of war his father still disapproved. When asked why, he told his wife, "To fight war entails fatal danger, but Zhao Kuo passed it off as something easy in his talk. It would be better if our king did not appoint him as commander. If he does, he will surely be the one to lead our troops to doom." When Zhao Kuo took over command he set about restructuring the army, reissuing orders and rules, and dismissing many senior officers. When the Qin general heard of this he attacked. Using the strategy *Lure the Tiger Down the Mountain* he faked a retreat. Zhao, overconfident and self-assured, assumed the retreat to be real and abandoned his fortifications to give chase. The Qin then circled back and destroyed the Zhao supply depot. Forty days later the Zhao troops were starving. Zhao Kuo and his personal guard made a last stand against the Qin, but were brought down in a hail of arrows. The Qin general knew that a seasoned general would never fall for such an obvious tactic, but playing on the younger general's weakness, he succeeded in neutralizing their initial advantage.[1]

WARRING STATES PERIOD CHINA

Almost thirty one years later, in 228 B.C., Qin was again attacking Zhao, but for the last time. During the previous years Qin had continued to expand, eating up smaller kingdoms on its borders. Once a mighty state, Zhao had been reduced to bribing Qin with territory as it frantically tried to buy time to rebuild its army. Zhao's only hope lay in the prowess of its leading general, Li Mu, to rally the remaining troops and devise some stratagem to save them from almost certain annihilation. The equally famous Qin general Wang Jian schemed to remove the pillar of the Zhao state through court intrigue. Now, it was known that King Yu of Zhao kept a homosexual lover by the name of Han Cang to whom he turned for advice in running the state. Han Cang was jealous of General Li's acclaim and eagerly accepted a bribe from Qin to slander Li, saying he was conspiring with Qin to commit treason. General Li was summoned to court where Han Cang read out the charges. "You were seen in the presence of the king with a dagger concealed in your sleeve. Thus you must have been plotting assassination. The penalty is execution!"

"But what you saw up my sleeve was not the handle of a dagger, but a splint for my crippled arm," replied Li Mu. "My left arm is crippled and weak. When kneeling at court I have difficulty rising and, since I do not wish to cause a distraction before his Majesty, I bound a splint to my arm so that I could rise without difficulty."

But Han Cang was not swayed, he said, "My instructions are to have you executed without argument. There

1. From RECORDS OF THE GRAND HISTORIAN.

will be no pardon. However, as a concession I will allow you to commit suicide."[2]

Li Mu bowed gratefully and retired from the audience chamber to fall upon his sword. However his crippled arm would not extend far enough to allow him to hold the tip to his belly, so he placed the sword in his mouth, dashed against a pillar, and killed himself. Five months later Qin attacked and Zhao was destroyed forever.[3]

SIX DYNASTIES PERIOD CHINA

In the year 383 Emperor Fu Jian of Qin personally led a cavalry of five thousand mounted soldiers to attack General Xie Shi of Jin. Discovering that the Jin forces were greater than he anticipated, the emperor had his army form defensive positions along the bank of the river. The Jin armies likewise encamped on the opposite side. Neither side wished to cross first, since it was well known that an army is most vulnerable when crossing a river. General Shi sent an envoy across the river with a message that read, "My lord, your army has entered deeply into our territory, and in deploying your ranks you have crowded upon the river. This is the plan for a lengthy stalemate. Do you really want to fight? If you will order your men to withdraw to a safe distance and allow us to cross we can then fight it out and settle the matter quickly."

The emperor agreed to the request. When his advisors objected Emperor Fu Jian told them that he planned to turn his army about and attack the Jin after half their troops had crossed. But General Xie anticipated the emperor's treachery and sent scouts disguised as imperial troops to infiltrate the Qin ranks. When the

---

2. Since punishments for treason in those times were particularly gruesome.

3. From the ZHAN GUO CE.

emperor ordered his army to pull back, the disguised Jin troops began to incite panic by spreading the rumor that Qin was withdrawing in defeat and that Jin was in hot pursuit. The retreat quickly turned into a rout as the Qin troops broke formation to escape. The emperor and his generals raced frantically after the fleeing soldiers with whips in hand to stop them, but to no avail. The Jin army quickly crossed the river and pursued the Qin forces, inflicting enormous casualties. The emperor was wounded and narrowly escaped. He was captured and strangled a few weeks later.[4]

SUMMARY

Commanding a large body of men is like dealing with an unthinking beast: its actions are not determined so much by what is logical as by circumstance of terrain and habit. An army that is invincible in a certain formation can be useless if that formation is broken. By changing the rules and habits under which the enemy is used to fighting, you take away his physical and moral foundation.

4. From THE CHRONICLE OF FU JIAN.

CHAPTER TWENTY-SIX

第二十六計

指桑罵槐

POINT AT THE MULBERRY BUT CURSE THE LOCUST TREE

Under hurtful accusations often lies a weak case.
—**CHINESE PROVERB**

A lie told by one, becomes truth when told by hundreds.
—**CHINESE PROVERB**

To discipline, control, or warn others whose status or position excludes them from direct confrontation, use analogy and innuendo. Without directly naming names, those accused cannot retaliate without revealing their complicity.

SPRING AND AUTUMN PERIOD CHINA

Duke Jing of Qi appointed Sima Rangchu as general of the army to lead the soldiers against Qin. Sima said, "I was formerly lowly and menial. If my lord pulls me out from my village and places me above the high officials, the officers and troops will not be submissive and the 'Hundred Surnames'[1] will not believe in me. Since I am insignificant and my authority light, I would like to have one of my lord's favored ministers, someone whom the state respects, as supervisor of the army. Then it will be possible." Duke Jing consented and appointed Zhuang Jia as supervisor. Sima met with Zhuang Jia and they agreed that they would begin the march at midday the next day. Sima went on ahead to the army camp where he gave orders to prepare for the next day's departure. He also ordered his guards to place a water clock in the parade grounds.

The next day Zhuang, who had always been arrogant and aristocratic, assumed that since Sima was already at the army camp and preparations were underway, it was not urgent for him to be there. His friends and relatives from all around gathered to detain him with drinks and entertainment. By midday Zhuang had still not arrived so Sima gave orders for the army to depart. By evening Zhuang had finally caught up with the army. Sima asked, "How is it that you arrived after the appointed time?"

Zhuang acknowledged his fault saying, "High officials and relatives saw this simple one off, thus I was detained."

Sima said, "On the day a general receives the mandate of command, he forgets his home; when he enters

---

1. An expression used to designate the Chinese people. There is reputed to have been one hundred tribes that emigrated into China in the third millennium B.C. They are considered the ancestors of the modern Chinese.

the army and takes control of the soldiers, he forgets his loved ones; when he takes hold of the drum sticks and urgently beats the drum, he forgets himself. At present, enemy states have already deeply invaded our lands, while within the state there is unrest and movement. Officers and soldiers lie brutally cut down and exposed on the borders. The fate of the entire population hangs upon you, so what do you mean by being seen off?"

Zhuang was speechless.

Sima then summoned the provost marshal and inquired, "What is the army's law regarding those who arrive after the appointed time?" He replied, "They should be beheaded!" Zhuang was terrified and sent a messenger racing back to the capital to have the duke issue an immediate pardon. But before the messenger returned with the pardon, Zhuang had already been executed. Thereafter the officials and nobles were all terrified of Sima and no one dared hesitate in following his orders.[2]

HAN DYNASTY CHINA

After Gaozu had become emperor he invested many of his followers. One day, while he was strolling along the balcony of his palace in Luoyang, he noticed several ministers milling about below speaking in hushed tones. "What are they talking about?" he asked his advisor, Zhang Liang. "Your majesty does not know?" replied Zhang. "They are plotting a revolt."

---

2. From the ZUO ZHUAN. The saying "when a man goes to war he forgets his wife and family" is well-known throughout Asia. After all, if one's army is dreaming about their homes and wives they are more likely to desert, a constant concern to the ancient generals. There is a story of an old 16th Century Japanese warrior who led a division of the Takeda army into battle accompanied by his youngest son. The son turned proudly towards his father and announced, "Now I am going into battle, I forget my wife and family!" But the father was not impressed and turned to his son and said. "A true samurai cannot possibly forget his wife and family when he goes into battle, because a true samurai never thinks of them at any time!"

"But peace and order have just been restored to the empire. Why should they be planning a revolt?"

"When your majesty rose from among the common people, it was through these men that you seized control of the empire. You have become the Son of Heaven, but those whom you have invested have all been close friends from the old days, while you have had your enemies of former times executed. Now these officers of your army, reckoning up the merits they have won, believe that there is not sufficient land in the whole empire to invest them all. So, some of them fear they will not receive their just allotment, while others tremble, lest, falling under suspicion for some error of their past, they be condemned to execution. Therefore they gather together in this way and plot rebellion."

"What should I do?" asked the emperor.

"Among all your followers whom do you dislike the most?" inquired Zhang Liang.

"Yong Chi and I are ancient enemies," replied the emperor. "Many times in the past he has brought me trouble and shame. I would like to have killed him, but because his merit is great, I have not had the heart."

"You must hurry and invest Yong Chi before anyone else, and make known what you have done to your other followers. When they see Yong Chi has been invested, they will all feel assured of their own rewards," said Zhang Liang.

The emperor agreed and held a feast to bestow Yong Chi with lands and titles. When the other ministers left the banquet they said to each other happily, "If even Yong Chi can become a marquis, the rest of us have nothing to worry about!"[3]

---

3. From RECORDS OF THE GRAND HISTORIAN.

HAN DYNASTY CHINA

In 195 B.C. Gaozu, the founder of the Han Dynasty, died. His wife, the Dowager Empress Lu, thereupon set about seizing power for herself and her clan. First, she had two princes assassinated, a third driven to suicide, and their kingdoms handed over to members of her own family. The empress also disposed of numerous ministers and advisors, not to mention all the former concubines of her late husband. Then she placed an infant on the throne claiming it to be the son of Gaozu when in fact she had stolen the infant and had the mother executed to cover the affair. The emperor's family line of Liu was in danger of being eclipsed by the newly powerful Lu clan. One marquis of the imperial line, Liu Chang, was embittered that his family was effectively ousted from holding position at court, and was determined to resist the empress's designs. Once, at a banquet held at the palace, the empress appointed Liu Chang to act as master of wine. This was meant as an insult, being asked to serve at a banquet, but Liu Chang did not show any offense. He asked the empress, "Since I come from a family of generals, I would like to direct the dispensing of wine in accordance with the rules of the army." The empress, unaware of the ramifications, gave her consent.

When the banquet was at its height Liu Chang poured wine for the empress and asked permission to sing a folk song that he learned as a child. The empress gave her permission and Liu Chang began to recite:

> *Deep we plough and thick we sow the seed;*
> *We set out the little plants where they will have room to grow.*
> *Whatever comes up that is not from our seed,*
> *We hoe it out and throw it away!*

The empress was outraged at the obvious allusion, but she could say nothing without admitting her resemblance to it. Later a member of the entourage became drunk and slipped away from the party without seeking permission from the empress. Liu Chang followed the man and drew his sword and slew him. Liu Chang returned to the party carrying the severed head and said to the startled guests, "Some man tried to desert the banquet! In accordance with army regulations I have duly carried out the penalty of execution!"

The empress and her courtiers were completely dumbfounded, but since the empress had given permission to conduct the service according to military protocol, no one could find fault with Liu's actions. Thereafter Liu Chang was treated with great deference by the court. Shortly after empress Lu passed away, the Liu clan revolted and, in keeping with the song, wiped out the entire Lu clan, except for one princess who was married to a marquis in a distant province.[4]

SUMMARY

A rule of leadership states to always reward in public but to criticize in private. However, there are times when others need to see the possible consequences of their behavior by making an example of someone.

---

4. From RECORDS OF THE GRAND HISTORIAN.

CHAPTER TWENTY-SEVEN

第二十七計

假痴不癲

FEIGN MADNESS, BUT KEEP YOUR BALANCE

It is the gnarled and crooked tree that escapes the woodsman's axe.

—LAO ZI

When an eagle is about to attack, it will fly low and draw in its wings. When a fierce cat is about to strike, it will fold back its ears and crouch low. When the Sage is about to move, he will certainly display a stupid countenance.

—THE SIX SECRET TEACHINGS OF THE TAI GONG

Hide behind the mask of a fool, a drunk, or a madman to create confusion about your intentions and motivations. Lure your opponent into underestimating your ability until, overconfident, he drops his guard. Then you may attack.

WARRING STATES PERIOD CHINA

Sun Bin was making a reputation for himself after graduating from the mysterious Ghost Valley School[1] when he was invited to become an advisor to the king of Wei. Another advisor at the court, Pang Juan, became jealous of Sun Bin's increasing popularity with the king and devised a scheme to frame Sun as a traitor. He convinced Sun that he should write to his family and plan a return trip home to show off his success. Sun was concerned about taking a leave from the court so soon after his appointment, but Pang reassured him that this was customary in Wei. Sun complied and wrote a letter to his family announcing his forthcoming visit. Pang had the letter intercepted and brought it to the king explaining that, since Sun had only spent three months at court, his imminent return could only mean that he was a spy and was planning to return with state secrets. The king was outraged and he had Sun imprisoned and the tendons behind his knees cut, hence Sun's first name Bin, meaning "crippled."

A year later Sun heard that an emissary from his home state would be visiting Wei, and he planned to escape. First, he feigned madness to relax the guard's vigil. He rubbed his own feces over his body and alternately screamed and wept, and then convulsed with laughter. Pang suspected this to be an act and so he tested him by placing a bowl of food and a bowl of feces through the bars. Sun ignored the delicious food and ate the contents of the other bowl instead. Convinced Sun had truly gone insane, Pang and the prison guards soon forgot about the "mad" prisoner. When the embassy

---

1. One of numerous rustic martial arts academies that sprang up during those times to train men in the arts of war. Disciples were pitted against each other in solving Taoist riddles, playing war games, and hand-to-hand combat.

from Yue arrived they received a secret message detailing Sun's plight. Determined to rescue their fellow countrymen they sought permission to visit with the famous but now insane strategist. The king gave his consent and, since the guards paid little attention, they were able to switch Sun for a double who volunteered to take his place. Sun was secretly spirited back to Yue where he went on to conquer Wei and kill Pang Juan using another famous tactic (see Chapter 28).[2]

Sui Dynasty China

During the final years of Emperor Yang of the Sui dynasty there appeared a ballad that foretold the fall of the house of Sui and the ascent of a man named Li as emperor. The ballad became immensely popular among the disaffected subjects of Emperor Yang's infamous rule. The emperor, being superstitious and believing in the prophesy himself, began a campaign to search out and execute anyone of importance with the surname Li. He had numerous ministers and officials along with their entire families put to the sword. A minor official by the name of Li Yuan was serving as superintendent in the provinces when he was summoned to the court. Li Yuan delayed appearing in court by claiming poor health. Li Yuan had a niece who was a palace maid. One day the emperor asked her where her uncle Li had been. The lady replied that her uncle was ill. The emperor said, "I wonder if he is courting death?" When Li Yuan got word of this he was certain that if he obeyed the summons to court he would never return. Thereupon he feigned madness and pretended to become an incorrigible drunk. When the imperial spies reported Li's behavior the emperor thought that a madmen could never fulfill the prophesy and was no longer suspicious of Li.

---

2. From RECORDS OF THE GRAND HISTORIAN.

Surprisingly, two years later the Sui emperor placed Li in charge of a field army to defend the empire against barbarian incursions. Li fought bravely, won the respect of his troops, marched on the capital, and went on to found the illustrious Tang dynasty, thus fulfilling the prophecy.[3]

MING DYNASTY CHINA

Just before his death in 1398, the founder of the Ming dynasty, Hongwu, bequeathed that the throne be passed over his sons to his grandson Huidi. Only sixteen when he was appointed emperor, Huidi was counseled by treacherous advisors to eliminate the other branches of the family. One by one the young emperor's uncles were summoned to court to answer to charges of corruption. Always found guilty, they were stripped of their rank, reduced to the status of commoner, and exiled to a remote district. One of the uncles, the prince of Shang, refused the summons and, in protest, set fire to his palace, burning his family to death. Then, mounting his terrified horse, he charged into the fire to his meet his own death. A year later five of the princes had been eliminated, leaving only one uncle that still retained position in the government: the prince of Yan. The prince was alone and isolated, waiting for the inevitable summons to court which he could not refuse since, in keeping with tradition, his own sons were held as hostages in the capital. To give himself time to plan a way of saving himself, he feigned madness. He ran through the streets of Beijing screaming and yelling, stealing food and wine, and sleeping in gutters. For days he sank into deep depressions and would see no one. In

---

3. Li Yuan first became king of Jin and assumed the throne name of Zhuangzong. He is again the main character in the third story of Chapter 28. From CHIU TANG-SHU CHI. Source: THE FOUNDING OF THE TANG DYNASTY.

warm weather he sat by the stove, shivering and com-
plaining of the cold. But it was all a smoke screen meant
to deceive the emperor. When the emperor heard these
reports he said, "Alas, my poor uncle has gone truly
insane. Let us release his sons to him in the hope that
they may bring him back to reason." This was the young
emperor's fatal mistake. With his sons safe, the prince of
Yan was free to openly challenge the emperor's authority. He raised an army and by 1402 the young emperor
was dead and the prince of Yan assumed the throne as
Emperor Yongle, one of the Ming dynasty's greatest
rulers.[4]

SUMMARY

It is well known that the strongest contender in any
sphere of activity automatically fears, and therefore
becomes an enemy to the second strongest. To hide
your strength, feign madness since without the power of
rational thought, all other powers are useless. When
you cease being a threat, hostile attentions will be
focused on the next most powerful. This buys you time
to scheme for victory.

4. From WHEN CHINA RULED THE SEAS.

CHAPTER TWENTY-EIGHT

第二十八計

上屋抽梯

LURE YOUR ENEMY ONTO THE ROOF, THEN TAKE AWAY THE LADDER

Avoid terrain that features cliffs and crags, narrow passes, tangled bush, and quagmires.

While avoiding such places ourselves, try to lure the enemy into such areas so that when we attack the enemy will have this type of terrain at his rear.

—SUN ZI

With baits and deceptions, lure your enemy into treacherous terrain. Then cut off his lines of communication and avenue of escape. To save himself he must fight both your own forces and the elements of nature.

WARRING STATES PERIOD CHINA

In 341 B.C. Wei was attacking Han, which in turn appealed to Qi for assistance. The king of Qi sought the advice of Sun Bin who recommended waiting until both armies were exhausted before intervening. To insure Han would put up a good defense, Sun sent messengers saying that an army was being readied and would be there at the first opportunity. After several weeks reports came in that both armies were weary of the siege and Sun again set out for the capital of Wei, an apparent repeat of his earlier strategy *Besiege Wei to Rescue Chao* (see Chapter 2). When the general of Wei, Pang Juan, heard that Sun had crossed into Wei he was furious. He then sent his army to catch up with them before they reached the capital. This time Pang was not going to allow himself to be ambushed, so he sent scouting parties well ahead of the main army. Having outfoxed Pang twice before, Sun's generals wondered how they could bait him into another trap. Sun said, "I know Pang Juan has a low opinion of the Qi soldiers and believes them to be cowards. We will allow him to believe this." Sun ordered that when his men encamped the first night they build one fire for every man, and on the next night, one fire for every two men, and on the third night, one fire for every three men. When Pang was within a few days march of the Qi forces he questioned his scouts who had been spying on the Qi army since it entered their territory. They reported that on the first night one hundred thousand fires were lit, on the second night only fifty thousand fires were lit, and on the third night only thirty thousand fires had been lit. Pang concluded that the deeper the Qi army penetrated Wei territory, the more their men became frightened and deserted. "They have heard I am here and they are fleeing in fear of my presence," declared Pang. One of his advisors was not so convinced and warned, "But the men of Qi are notorious for their trickery we should be careful before pursuing them recklessly." However, Pang did not heed his advice.

Meanwhile Sun found the perfect terrain to stage an ambush: a stretch of road that was flanked by hills and woods. In these woods he concealed his archers and, at the entrance of the valley, he had them build a rough defensive barrier. About seven hundred yards further along the trail there was a large oak tree. Sun peeled off the tree's bark and wrote in large characters: "Pang Juan will die here." He gave instructions that the archers should lie in waiting throughout the night and, when they saw a light appear near the tree, shoot towards the light. As expected, Pang arrived at the entrance of the valley shortly after dark and first encountered the defensive obstruction. He laughed telling his men this was but a desperate trick of a fleeing enemy. He ordered the barrier torn down and was proceeding along the road when a scout reported that something had been written on a tree up ahead. Pang went to investigate for himself. He ordered a torch brought up so that he could better read the characters. When the light of the torch shone on the tree, Sun's hidden archers rained five thousand arrows towards it killing everyone in the vanguard and wounding Pang Juan. Knowing he was beaten, Pang cut his own throat. His last words were, "That upstart. Now with my death I've made his reputation!"[1] And it did. Sun Bin went on to write a famous book on strategy called, THE ART OF WARFARE. The book was lost for almost two thousand years until recently rediscovered in a Han dynasty tomb.

---

1. From RECORDS OF THE GRAND HISTORIAN.

HAN DYNASTY CHINA

After defeating the rebel kingdom of Wei, the famous Han general Han Xin was sent to quell the other two kingdoms who had revolted, Qi and Chu. General Han set out towards Qi, but Chu sent its general, Long Chu, with a force of two hundred thousand men to intercept Han's invasion of Qi. The two armies met on opposite sides of the Wei River. General Han ordered his men to fill over ten thousand sandbags and carry them up-river to dam the flow of water. The next morning General Han led his army across the lowered river and attacked Chu, but after a short engagement pretended defeat and fled back across the river. General Long announced, "See, I always knew Han Xin was a coward!" and he led his army across the river in pursuit. Through a pre-arranged signal, General Han had his men break the dam and free the pent-up waters. Only half of the Chu army was across the river when the flood cut the army in half, drowning those caught midstream. General Han then wheeled around his retreating forces and attacked the advance guard of Chu, killing General Long Chu. The remaining troops panicked and fled in all directions, but in the end were captured by the pursuing Han soldiers.[2]

SUI DYNASTY CHINA

In A.D. 910 King Zhuangzong of Jin,[3] the future Tang emperor, set out to rescue the ally state of Zhou from the invading Liang forces. The Jin forces were outnumbered by the Liang, but they had more cavalry, while the Liang army consisted of mostly infantry and new recruits. The Liang set up defensive fortifications along the river in wooded terrain flanked by marshes and

2. From RECORDS OF THE GRAND HISTORIAN.

3. Known by his birth name, Li Yuan, in Chapter 27.

awaited the Jin. The Jin army was far from base and supplies were thin. King Chuang needed to fight a decisive battle quickly or risk being starved into submission, but General Zhou warned against a frontal attack on the Liang. He said, "The people of Liang excel at fighting from fortified defense and are not adept at open field combat, while our own strength lies with our cavalry. Now cavalry are adept at warfare on open plains and expansive wilds, but our army is encamped in wetlands and forest. This is hardly terrain that would be advantageous to us. It would be better to withdraw the army to Haoyi and thereby entice the enemy to leave their encampment." The king agreed and they withdrew the army. Then General Zhou led a thousand cavalry to provoke skirmishes with Liang's encampment. Enraged, the Liang came forth with all their troops and fought running battles with General Zhou that eventually stretched several dozen miles. General Zhou and King Chuang watched the battle from the top of a nearby hill. The king said, "The Liang have been lured onto level plains and shallow grass—our cavalry can advance and withdraw unhindered. Truly this is terrain where we can wrest victory." He ordered General Zhou to attack, but the general replied, "Without any preparation Liang's forces hastily came forth and have now traveled far. Moreover, they certainly did not have any time to prepare rations. Even if they did, they would not have had the leisure to eat them. By midday their men will be hungry and thirsty, and their army will certainly withdraw. If we attack them while they are withdrawing, we will inevitably be victorious." By late afternoon the Liang forces were seen pulling back. General Zhou ordered the beating of the drums, and with a tumultuous clamor advanced to attack. Exhausted and cutoff from supplies, the Liang forces suffered a serious defeat.[4]

---

4. From THE FOUNDING OF THE TANG DYNASTY.

SUMMARY

Every type of terrain can provide both an advantage for one form of warfare while a hindrance for another. A large force has the advantage in open terrain, while it is hindered by the narrow. But a small force is vulnerable in open spaces, yet protected by the narrow. Therefore, the key is to lure your enemy onto a terrain that hinders his abilities while helping your own.

第二十九計

樹上開花

Tie Silk Blossoms to the Dead Tree

Spreading out pennants and making the flags conspicuous are the means by which to cause doubt in the enemy. Analytically positioning the fences and screens is the means by which to bedazzle and make the enemy doubtful.

—Sun Bin

Tying silk blossoms on a dead tree gives the illusion that the tree is healthy. Through the use of artifice and disguise make something of no value appear valuable; of no threat appear dangerous; of no use, useful.

HAN DYNASTY CHINA

During the later Han dynasty, the Qiang barbarians revolted and invaded Han territory. The Empress Dowager Teng appointed General Yu Xu to raise an army and drive out the barbarians. The Qiang led several thousand troops to occupy the strategic pass of Yaoku to await the Han. Outnumbered, General Yu halted his army some distance from the pass and publicly announced that he would wait until reinforcements arrived before venturing any further. When the Qiang heard this they relaxed their formations and divided up into raiding parties to plunder the local countryside. Taking advantage of their scattering, General Yu broke through the pass and advanced at double the normal speed covering more than a hundred *li* a day. The Qiang regrouped to give chase, but the Han already had a day's head start on them. General Yu sought to dissuade the Qiang from attacking. On the first night he ordered his soldiers to light one cooking fire for every man. On the second night each man was to light two cooking fires, and on the third, three. Seeing that the number of cooking fires increased each night the Qiang did not dare to attack. Someone asked, "Sun Bin reduced his cooking fires but you increased them (see Chapter 28). Furthermore, according to THE ART OF WAR, an army on the march should not exceed thirty *li* a day, yet today you have advanced a hundred. Why is this?" Yu replied, "The enemy troops are numerous while our soldiers are few. When the barbarians see our fires increasing each day they will certainly interpret it as evidence that reinforcements from the garrison are joining us. Believing that our numbers are many while our speed is quick, they will hesitate to pursue us. Sun Bin manifested weakness, but I now display strength because our relative strategic power is different." The Qiang became ever more wary of engaging in battle and finally decided to disperse and return to their homelands. It was then that General Yu turned about and pursued the retreating barbarians inflicting severe causalities and driving them out of the territory.[1]

THREE KINGDOMS PERIOD CHINA

Duke Zhou Yu asked assistance from Liu Bei in his plans for attacking their mutual enemy Cao Cao. Liu Bei lent the duke the famous strategist Kong Ming to assist with his planning. The duke however became miffed with Kong Ming because of his outspoken and usually contrary opinions. The duke wanted to execute him but another minister, Lu Su, intervened and said that they could not outright execute an advisor without just cause, as this would destroy their alliance with Liu Bei. The duke conceded and decided to set up Kong Ming for a failure, after which, Kong would be forced to commit suicide. The duke called all his generals to counsel. In front of these witnesses the duke turned to Kong and asked, "Renowned advisor, in several days Cao Cao will arrive and we will do battle along the river and its environs, what do you believe to be the most important weapon for such an engagement?"

Kong Ming replied, "For river combat, the bow and arrow are the most important."

"I cannot agree with you more," said the duke. "But we are in short supply, I wonder then if you will oversee the production of one hundred thousand arrows to be delivered within ten days."

Kong Ming sensed the trap. To produce ten thousand arrows a day was a near impossible task, should he fail to produce the arrows within the appointed time he would be forced to commit suicide. Not to be outdone however he replied, "Cao Cao's forces may arrive any

---

1. From UNORTHODOX STRATEGIES.

day, ten days is too long to wait, instead I shall deliver the arrows within three days."

The duke and his advisor Lu Su couldn't believe their luck for surely Kong Ming would fail to do in three days what was nearly impossible to do in ten. The next day Kong Ming did nothing but relax and stroll about the parks. The duke seeing this was impressed with Kong's dispassionate resolve to die, since it seemed he wasn't even trying to fulfill his promise. The second day Kong Ming secretly borrowed twenty river junks and had them outfitted by lining the hull, cabin walls, and gunwales with hundreds of bundles of straw.

Before daybreak on the third day, Kong Ming had the junks chained together. He woke up Lu Su and asked if he wished to accompany him as he went to pick up his shipment of one hundred thousand arrows. Lu Su, curious to see this for himself, agreed to go along. In the morning fog the ships slowly made their way up-river towards the encampment of Cao Cao. As the junks neared the camp they suddenly became visible to the startled Wei guards. They immediately alerted Cao Cao who, suspecting a surprise attack, ordered all his archers to rain arrows at the approaching fleet. As the junks made their way up past the enemy encampment the bundles of straw facing the enemy camp were filled with arrows. Kong Ming then turned the ships around and filled the other side with arrows as well before disappearing back into the fog. Cao Cao, fearing a trap, refused to let his naval commanders go after the retreating junks. When the junks returned to base the arrows collected exceeded more than one hundred thousand. When Lu Su made his report the duke said, "Alas, this man is superior to me." Kong Ming later became prime minister under the duke.[2]

---

2. From ROMANCE OF THE THREE KINGDOMS.

THREE KINGDOMS PERIOD CHINA

During the final years of the Three Kingdoms, Sima Yan usurped the throne of Wei, made himself king, and changed the name of the kingdom from Wei to Jin. News of this reached the neighboring king of Wu who knew that his kingdom would be the next likely target of the ambitious Sima. He worried so much that he died several days later. Sun Hao then inherited the throne of Wu and immediately took to pleasure and vice, neglecting state affairs. Over the next few years the new king of Wu grew increasingly paranoid and had dozens of his advisors and commanders and their entire families executed on the slightest suspicion. As a result he was widely reviled. Hearing that the people of Wu despised their king, Sima ordered a naval attack led by commander Wang Chun. The king of Wu had no idea of what to do against the impending naval attack. He convened what remained of his council and one advisor recommended stringing a bamboo barrier across the river to prevent the fleet from reaching the Wu capital of Jian Ye. The king agreed and heavy bamboo cords were made and strung just below the surface. When Commander Wang heard about the barrier he laughed. He ordered his men to build huge rafts from timbers on which were erected straw dummies dressed in armor and holding weapons. The dummies were soaked in oil and a trip mechanism was attached that would ignite the dummies when the rafts struck the barrier. The rafts burned through the bamboo and continued on down stream to the Wu capital. The spectacle of a fleet of rafts full of burning men so frightened the Wu troops that they fled in terror. Sima captured Wu and went on to found the short lived Jin dynasty.[3]

---

3. From ROMANCE OF THE THREE KINGDOMS.

SUMMARY

While it is important to learn of your enemy's plans, it is equally important to conceal your own. Through the use of props, facades, and camouflage, you keep the enemy in doubt of your strengths and weaknesses. Not knowing where to attack, the enemy is led to defeat.

CHAPTER THIRTY

第三十計

反客爲主

EXCHANGE THE ROLE OF GUEST FOR THAT OF HOST

The strategists have a saying: I dare not play the host, but play the guest; I dare not advance an inch, but retreat a foot instead. This is known as marching forward when there is no road, rolling up one's sleeve when there is no arm, dragging one's adversary by force when there is no adversary, and taking up arms when there are no arms.

—LAO ZI

Defeat the enemy from within by infiltrating the enemy's camp under the guise of cooperation, surrender, or peace treaties. In this way you can discover his weakness and then, when the enemy's guard is relaxed, strike directly at the source of his strength.

— **153** —

QIN DYNASTY CHINA

Xiang Liang came from a long line of Chu generals but the family lost power when the state of Chu was defeated and annexed by Qin. In his youth he had killed a man and escaped with his nephew Xiang Yu to the state of Wu requesting asylum from the governor. The governor welcomed Xiang Liang and gave him an administrative position. During this time Xiang secretly formed a band of guests and retainers and trained them in the art of war while establishing a reputation as a competent leader. Then in 209 B.C. the various states and kingdoms rose up in open revolt against the oppressive Qin dynasty. When word of the revolt reached Wu the governor saw an opportunity to improve his position by joining the rebellion. He called Xiang Liang and said, "All regions west of the Yangtze River are in revolt. The time has come when heaven will destroy the house of Qin. I have heard it said that "He who takes the lead may rule others, but he who lags behind will be ruled by others." I would like to dispatch an army with you and your nephew at the head." Xiang Liang, who took the advice in a way the governor would regret, said, "This is a great honor you have bestowed on my family and I beg leave to call in my nephew Yu, so that he may receive your orders directly." The governor consented. Xiang Liang went to summon his nephew and secretly gave him instructions to hold his sword in readiness. They returned to the governor and after some time Xiang Liang turned to his nephew and said, "You may proceed!" This was the signal, and without hesitation Yu drew his sword and cut off the governor's head in a single stroke. Xiang Liang then picked up the head, removed the governor's seals of office, and declared himself governor. The few attendants that objected were quickly attacked and killed by Yu so that no one else dared to oppose the appointment. Xiang Liang went on to rally several armies to his side in revolt against the Qin. After numerous victories he re-conquered his home state of Chu and became a contender for the emperor's throne before being killed in battle against another rival for the empire.[1]

HAN DYNASTY CHINA

In 180 B.C. empress Lu, the wife of the first Han emperor, passed away. For years after her husband's death she had held power, supplanting the authority of the late emperor's Liu clan with her own family, the Lü. Upon her death the Liu family plotted to reclaim their control over the empire. One of the few remaining members of the Liu clan who had escaped the empress's purge still held a high position as the king of Qi. He received a secret message asking him to raise his troops and march on the capital of Chang'an where he would be assisted by other Liu supporters from within. The king of Qi ordered his general, Wei Po, to secretly ready the army for mobilization, but the prime minister of Qi learned of the king's intentions. He intercepted the general's orders and, using the imperial seals in his possession, ordered the army to surround the king's palace and keep him prisoner until further instructions arrived from the capital.[2] General Wei Po went to speak with the prime minister, pretending that he had no involvement or knowledge of the king's plot, and said, "Even though the king wants to send out his troops, he cannot since he does not possess the Tiger Seals[3] of the Han court which

---

1. From RECORDS OF THE GRAND HISTORIAN.

2. The prime minister was appointed by the court to watch over the conduct of the king.

3. These were small cast bronze figurines of a tiger that was split in two pieces, "male" and "female," that fit together to make a whole. The king would keep one half, and his commanders, the other. A courier bearing orders would be given the complementary half. A comman-

would give him authority to do so. I beg you allow me to take command of the troops for you and keep the king under guard!"

The prime minister, believing that Wei Po was on his side, handed over the seals and put him in charge of the troops. But as soon as he had taken command, Wei Po had the troops surround the prime minister's offices instead.

"Alas!" said the prime minister. "The Daoists have a saying: 'Strike when the hour comes, or suffer the ruin that follows.' This, then is what they meant!" The prime minister then committed suicide. The remaining members of the Liu clan rose up in revolt and destroyed the entire Lü family.[4]

MING DYNASTY CHINA

During the Ming dynasty, in the Songjiang region, there lived a wealthy man known as Rich Man Pan. As rich as Pan was, he was always hungry for more and sought out every opportunity to make money. Having heard about alchemy Pan became obsessed with the idea of turning lead into gold and went to great expense inviting wandering sages and alchemists to his house to teach him the secret. Yet after more than ten years of experiments, Pan was still unable to convert even a gram of lead into gold. Meanwhile, Pan's interest in alchemy became known far and wide. One year Pan went on vacation in the luxurious resort town of West Lake just outside of Hangzhao. Pan's villa was large and sumptuous, but next door was an even grander villa. Over the weeks Pan observed his neighbor who appeared to be fabulously wealthy and who was accompanied by a stunningly attractive young woman. Pan contrived to

der, upon receiving an order, would check that the courier's half and his own fit together, thus insuring that the orders were genuine.

4. From RECORDS OF THE GRAND HISTORIAN.

meet this elegant stranger, and over the weeks they became acquainted. The man's name was Jia Wuzhi and Pan was anxious to find out the source of his wealth. After discreet questioning, Jia told Pan that he was an alchemist. Pan was stunned and told him of his own efforts in that field. Pan doubted that it was possible after all, but Jia chided his lack of faith and as a matter of honor offered to demonstrate his technique. He brought out a tripod which he set over a fire. Cradled on the tripod was a porcelain dish containing what appeared to be common lead. Jia heated the dish until the lead melted then, removing a silk bag from his person, he scooped out a small amount of black powder and mixed this with the molten lead. The lead instantly transformed into valuable silver. Pan was astonished and asked him how it was done. Jia explained that the process was long and costly but once the powder, called the "silver breeder," was produced it would transform enough lead into silver to make Pan the wealthiest man in China. Pan explained that he already had a laboratory set up at his home and he begged Jia to be his guest there and help him to create the silver breeder. "Well, since you have already studied the art yourself, it may be all right. But be warned that the rules are strict and I will only show you the process once," said the alchemist. When Jia and his beautiful wife arrived, Pan was stricken by the woman's beauty. Jia explained that the more silver used, the greater the potency, so Pan bought as much silver as he could get hold of, over four thousand taels. The next day they began. Jia explained that the process was one of purification and refinement and that both he and Pan must wash, fast, and avoid any activity that was impure. Most important, only he and Pan could enter the sacred area to attend the fire. But, in case of emergency, Jia's wife could substitute since she was specially trained for this job. The process would take eighty-one days to complete. Pan was warned not to look into the covered cauldron before the final day. A few days later a message arrived informing Jia that his mother was ill and that she requested his presence at her death bed. Jia explained the situation to Pan who was deeply concerned about the silver breeder, but Jia reassured him saying he would leave his wife behind to oversee the process. After Jia left, Pan grew ever more lustful for the alchemist's wife. One night in a fit of passion he seduced her in the sacred chamber. On the eighty first day, Jia returned and he and Pan went to inspect the boiler, but as soon as Jia opened the lid his facial expression turned to anger. "What has happened to the silver breeder?" he shouted. "Has anyone done anything here that could have affected the purity of the atmosphere?" Pan was shocked into silence. The alchemist summoned his wife and angrily asked her if anything had occurred in the room while he was gone. At first she denied everything, but after Jia grabbed a whip and threatened to beat her with it she confessed to the seduction. Jia was furious, he turned to Pan and said, "You greedy scoundrel! With all your money you could buy as many wives as you want, but you still wanted to defile my wife. Well, you have your just reward since the silver breeder has all evaporated. And I will never show you the secret now." Whereupon the alchemist and his wife left, ignoring Pan's pleas for forgiveness. Two years later the still brooding Pan returned to the West Lake area, but under more modest conditions. There, one day he spotted a woman who looked like the alchemist's wife. He questioned her and she did indeed recognize him. Pan asked about her husband and the woman replied, "Oh, I was never married. I was hired for three months to pretend to be the wife of an alchemist, but now I am working for another alchemist who is at this moment meeting with his new client."[5]

JAPANESE FOLK TALE

In feudal Japan there lived a venerable kendo master who decided to test his three highest ranking students. He brought them one by one to an old temple in the nearby mountains where he told each student, "You have studied with me many years, now lets see if my teaching has been in vain. There, within the temple, awaits your test. Pass and you will have graduated."

Within the dimly lit temple the Master had hidden four samurai armed with clubs and instructions to jump anyone who entered the temple. The first student entered the temple and, before his eyes could adjust to the light, he was surprised and beaten by the samurai.

"I am sorry, you have failed," said the master.

The second student entered the temple and sensed the attackers. He was able to deftly evade their attack and defeat them. The student came out of the temple triumphant, but again the master said, "I am sorry, you have failed.'

Finally, the third student was brought to the temple and told about the test. The student replied, "But venerable master, protocol dictates that when entering a temple the master must always precede the student, so if you please, I shall follow you in." To which the master replied, "You rascal! You have learned all I can teach you."[6]

---

5. From PAO-WEN LAO-JEN, Source: TRADITIONAL CHINESE STORIES.
6. From THE ZEN WAY TO THE MARTIAL ARTS.

SUMMARY

When you are weak but your enemy is strong there is no chance for victory in a direct contest. Instead, by assuming a subordinate position, you may have the chance of undermining and subverting your enemy's power.

CHAPTER THIRTY-ONE

第三十一計

美人計

THE STRATEGY OF
BEAUTIFUL WOMEN

Increase the enemy's excesses, seize what he loves. Then we, acting from without, can cause a response from within.
  —SIMA FA, SEVEN MILITARY CLASSICS

Assist [the enemy] in his licentiousness and indulgence in music in order to dissipate his will. Make him generous gifts of pearls, and jade, and ply him with beautiful women.
  —THE SIX SECRET TEACHINGS OF THE TAI GONG

Send your enemy beautiful women to cause discord within his camp. This strategy can work on three levels. First, the ruler becomes so enamored with the beauty that he neglects his duties and allows his vigilance to wane. Second, other males at court will begin to display aggressive behavior, which inflames minor differences, hinders cooperation, and destroys morale. Third, other females at court, motivated by jealousy and envy, begin to plot intrigues, further exasperating the situation.[1]

WARRING STATES PERIOD CHINA

A wandering strategist by the name of Chang Yi traveled to Chu in search of employment. By the time he arrived he was reduced to poverty. His attendant became angry and wanted to go back. Chang Yi said, "So you are dissatisfied wearing rags and you wish to return, but wait until I have had an audience with the king and see then if our fortunes have not changed."

The next day Chang Yi had an audience with the king who told him he had no need for another advisor, to which Chang Yi replied, "Since your majesty has no need for my services will he permit me to travel to Jin to seek employment there?"

"Granted," said the king.

Chang Yi said, "Is there anything that I can procure for the king while I am in Jin?"

The king sneered and said, "Gold, pearls, gems, rhinoceros horn, and ivory are all available here. What does Jin have that I could possibly want?"

"Ah, so the king is not interested in beautiful women?"

"Why do you say that?"

"Because the women of Jin are renowned for their beauty and grace. Those who see them for the first time believe them to be goddesses."

---

1. Women can be used in a number of ways: as direct influence through the target's affections for a woman, sexual extortion, as a means of gather information through bedroom talk, and as blackmail by threatening to expose infidelity to wives and the public, known in modern spy parlance as the "honey trap."

"Well, if this is true we would be most interested in seeing such beauties." Having said that, the king provided Chang Yi with pearls and jade with which to purchase a few girls.

At that time the king's two favorite wives, Queen Nan and the concubine Zheng Xiu, heard about Chang Yi's mission to Jin and were very much afraid. They both sent agents to him, each bearing five hundred catties of gold and a letter which read, "We have heard of your mission to Jin and have sent you a thousand catties of gold that you may use to cover the costs of your journey."

The next day before Chang Yi was to depart he went to the king to say his farewell. Chang Yi asked permission to offer a toast to his majesty and the king agreed. After the first toast Chang Yi said, "Is there no one who can join us in a toast to your majesty's health?"

"If you wish, I will call in my favorites to join us," replied the king, and he summoned Queen Nan and Zheng Xiu. When they entered the room Chang Yi took one look and then prostrated himself before the king saying, "I have committed a mortal offense against your Majesty."

"How so?" asked the king.

"I have traveled throughout the empire and seen countless beauties, but never have I seen two women as beautiful as these. So, when I said I would get your Majesty real beauties, I unintentionally deceived you."

"You are pardoned," said the king. "I always felt that in all the empire there were no women as beautiful as these." The king allowed Chang Yi to keep the money he gave him and, along with the gold given by the king's women, Chang Yi became quite wealthy and found a suitable appointment with another king.[2]

---

2. From the ZHAN GUO CE.

HAN DYNASTY CHINA

In 199 B.C. the Han emperor, Gaozu, personally led his army against the invading Xiongnu. The emperor, however, was no match against the cunning tribesmen and he was led into a trap and suffered heavy losses (see Chapter 15). He and his remaining forces retreated to the city of Pingcheng for refuge, but were surrounded by some three hundred thousand horsemen. There the emperor remained surrounded for seven days with no possibility of bringing in either provisions or reinforcements. The emperor thought there was nothing left to do but surrender when his advisor, Chen Ping, came up with another strategy. Chen had a painting made of a beautiful Chinese princess which he secretly delivered to the wife of the Xiongnu commander. Along with the painting he sent a message that read, "My emperor intends to surrender to your husband, and so, to win his favor he is sending him a present of one of China's famous beauties to be his concubine." When the Xiongnu commander's wife saw the painting and read the note she was mad with jealousy. Fearing that such a beautiful rival would steal her husband's affections, she persuaded her husband to lift the siege and return home. The next morning when the emperor awoke he discovered the Xiongnu had left and he was able to return safely to his capital.[3]

THREE KINGDOMS PERIOD CHINA

The last Han emperor was under the dominion of the powerful warlord of Wei, Dong Zhuo. He was a ruthless man who was in the habit of executing senior ministers and officials if they should disagree with his opinions. The governor of Wei, Wang Yun, knew it was only a matter of time before his head was on the chopping

---

3. From HISTORY OF THE FORMER HAN DYNASTY.

block as well. He spent many sleepless nights wondering how to rid the kingdom of this tyrant. One night he was approached by his household sing-song girl known as Sable Cicada who offered to help Wang bring down the tyrant Dong. Wang was touched by the girl's sincerity and agreed to use her in the *Strategy of Beautiful Women*. Now, it so happened that Dong Zhuo's second in command was a young and valiant warrior by the name of Lu Bu. Dong had adopted the popular commander as his son as a means of sealing both the youth's, and the army's loyalty. One day, Wang invited Lu Bu to a gracious feast at his villa where he was wined, dined, and entertained by dancers and singers. As the evening progressed Wang called for another pot of wine which was brought in and served by the stunning Sable Cicada. The more Lu Bu drank, the more enamored he became with Sable, until he asked his host who she was. Wang told him Sable was his niece and if the commander so desired, he could have her as his wife. Lu Bu was most grateful and Wang assured him that he would arrange a day for the wedding and send Sable to him at his palace.

A few days later Wang invited the warlord Dong Zhuo to his villa for dinner and entertainment. After they had drunk several pots of wine, the beautiful Sable was brought out to dance. Dong Zhuo was infamous for his sexual appetite and the instant he saw Sable he was stricken with desire. Wang, seeming to notice the general's interest, offered him his "little household maid" to be his concubine. The general happily accepted the offer and carried Sable off in his carriage that very night. The next morning Lu Bu visited Wang to inquire about Sable. Wang told him the terrible news that Dong Zhuo, hearing of Lu Bu's impending marriage to his niece, came over to see if she met with his approval.

Upon seeing how beautiful she was he took her for himself. Wang pitifully explained that he was in no position to refuse the desires of such a powerful warlord. Lu Bu was enraged and secretly went to visit Sable at Dong's palace. Sable confirmed Wang's story, and said that, although she loved Lu Bu and hated the old tyrant, there was nothing she could do. Lu Bu continued to secretly visit Sable over several weeks. By this time Dong Zhuo, who was also completely taken with Sable, started to have suspicions about the constant presence of his second-in-command. One day he happened upon the two of them talking in the garden and in a fit of jealousy chased Lu Bu with a spear. When he questioned Sable about what was going on and she told him that Lu Bu had been pestering her for weeks and was about to rape her when he arrived in time to chase him away. Dong Zhuo wanted to execute Lu Bu immediately, but his senior minister intervened saying that to do so would undermine the already shaky morale of the army. So, Dong delayed the order. Lu Bu was sulking in the woods when he happened upon Wang Yun. He told Wang the terrible sequence of events and Wang replied that truly Dong Zhuo was a tyrant and a traitor to the emperor for usurping his power. Together they plotted his assassination. They forged an invitation from the emperor for Dong Zhuo to visit the capital where they prepared a trap. Upon entering the emperor's palace Dong had to present his weapons to the gate keeper. Once inside the palace he was attacked and killed by Lu Bu and his men. Lu Bu then assumed the title of General, had Dong's property confiscated, and every Dong family member executed. Lu Bu married Sable who was a good wife to him.[4]

---

4. From ROMANCE OF THE THREE KINGDOMS.

SUMMARY

The power of a beautiful woman is her ability to arouse intense feelings in those around her. Lust, jealousy, envy, and hatred are powerful emotions that create an atmosphere in which rational thought becomes impossible. This is psychological warfare at it most insidious.

CHAPTER THIRTY-TWO

第三十二計

空城計

THE STRATEGY OF OPEN CITY GATES

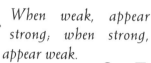

When weak, appear strong; when strong, appear weak.

—SUN ZI

One who excels as a warrior does not appear formidable; One who excels in defeating the enemy does not join issue. This is known as the virtue of non contention.

—LAO ZI

When the enemy is superior in numbers and your situation is such that you expect to be overrun at any moment, then drop all pretense of military preparedness and act casually. Unless the enemy has an accurate description of your situation, this unusual behavior will arouse suspicions. With luck he will be dissuaded from attacking.[1]

HAN DYNASTY CHINA

In 166 B.C. General Li Guang of the Han dynasty was out on patrol with a hundred cavalrymen when they spotted three Xiongnu horsemen on a scouting patrol. The Han cavalry gave chase killing two and capturing the third. On their return to their main camp they were spotted by several thousand Xiongnu horsemen in the distance. The troop commanders were all for making a run for it, but Li Guang knew they could never outride thousands of horsemen over a hundred kilometers to reach their main army. Instead of running away, Li Guang ordered his men to advance towards the enemy until they were within two kilometers. Then he ordered them to stop out in the open and dismount. He further ordered that all the horses be unsaddled and the men to relax and lie down in the grass. The Xiongnu sent scouts to investigate but Li Guang sent a few of his men out to chase them away. Watching from a distance, the Xiongnu commanders suspected that the Han patrol was a decoy and the rest of the army lay somewhere nearby waiting in ambush. The Xiongnu decided to stay and watch from a distance. That night they heard the Han soldiers singing and drinking, certainly not making any effort to escape. This seemed to convince the Xiongnu that the Han were using a clever ruse in order to launch a surprise night attack. The next morning Li Guang and his men discovered the Xiongnu had disappeared and they were able to leisurely make their way back to the main camp.[2]

---

1. This is the strategy of reverse psychology. Since Sun Zi's axiom "Appear strong when weak..." is so universally understood by generals from every age and culture, if you appear weak most commanders will assume you are just using an elementary strategy and that your maneuvers are but bait for a trap.

2. From RECORDS OF THE GRAND HISTORIAN.

THREE KINGDOMS PERIOD CHINA

In 149 B.C. the famous strategist Kong Ming of Shu , wishing to attack the state of Wei, sent an advance force to scout for the enemy. Leading the army of Wei was Sima Yi who also sent an advance force of fifty thousand troops. The two vanguards met and engaged in battle, but the Wei forces were superior and won the day. The defeated Shu vanguard raced back to the main body of Kong Ming's army whose troops, seeing the look of fear in the faces of their comrades, thought that the enemy was upon them and fled in panic. Kong Ming and a few bodyguards fled to the city of Yangping with the Wei army in hot pursuit. Vastly outnumbered and unable to either retreat or sustain a siege, Kong Ming played a last resort strategy that made him famous throughout China. He removed all the guards and battle flags from the walls and had all four of the city gates flung open. When Sima Yi approached the city he could see only a few old men nonchalantly sweeping the grounds within the gates. Kong Ming was seen sitting in one of the towers smiling and playing his lute. Sima Yi remarked to his advisors, "That man seems to be too happy for my comfort. Doubtless he has some deep laid scheme in mind to bring us all to disaster." As they stood spell bound, the strains of Kong Ming's lute reached their ears, and this only heightened their sense of foreboding. Such peculiar behavior was too suspicious. Fearing a clever trap, Sima Yi turned his army back and retreated. After the army left, Kong Ming and his remaining troops departed in the opposite direction and made their way safely back to their capital.[3]

---

3. From ROMANCE OF THE THREE KINGDOMS.

HOJO REGENCY JAPAN

During the battle of Mikatagahara in 1572 the Takeda army, led by Takeda Shingen, was planning to lay siege to Hamamatsu castle belonging to Tokugawa Ieyasu. To avoid being besieged and starved out by the vastly superior Takeda army, Iyasu prepared defensive positions three kilometers away in order to engage the Takeda before they could reach the castle. The battle was fiercely fought throughout the day, but by nightfall the Tokugawa forces were exhausted and were retreating for the castle with the Takeda giving chase. The commander of the castle wanted to close and bolt the city gates, but Iyasu interrupted him saying, "Closing the gates is exactly what Shingen is expecting. Then our remaining troops would be left out in the open where they would be hunted down one by one." Tokugawa ordered that the gates be left open and a huge brazier lit in front of the gates to guide the fleeing soldiers through the dark countryside. In addition, he ordered a large war drum to be beaten so that his troops could follow the sound until they saw the beacon. When the Takeda forces arrived at the castle to see the gates open and a brazier burning in front, Shingen immediately suspected a trap and ordered his troops to pull back. In this way Ieyasu was able to prevent the Takeda from attacking while allowing his remaining forces to find their way back to the safety of the castle.[4]

SUMMARY

In a desperate situation, often the only recourse is to do something completely unexpected. Unusual behavior in a time of crises arouses suspicions and doubts. Placing doubt in your enemy's mind means he is already half defeated. However, this strategy requires supreme self control. Those nervous about the chances for failure will, by their actions, give away the bluff.

---

4. From THE SAMURAI.

CHAPTER THIRTY-THREE

第三十三計

反間計

THE STRATEGY OF SOWING DISCORD

*Reduce the effectiveness of
your enemy by inflicting
discord among them.*
—SUN ZI

*Plans and projects for
harming the enemy are not
confined to any one method.
Sometimes entice his wise and virtuous
men away so that he has no counselors. Or send treacherous people to
his country to wreck his administra-
tion. Sometimes use cunning deceptions
to alienate his ministers from the sovereign. Or send skilled craftsmen to encour-
age the people to exhaust their wealth. Or present him with
licentious musicians and dancers to change his customs. Or
give him beautiful women to bewilder him.*

—JIA LIN

Undermine your enemy's ability to fight by secretly causing discord between him and his friends, allies, advisors, family, commanders, soldiers, and population. While he is preoccupied settling internal disputes, his ability to attack or defend is compromised.[1]

WARRING STATES PERIOD CHINA

Towards the end of the Warring States period, as the smaller kingdoms fell prey to the larger, the kingdom of Qin had become the single most powerful state. Qin posed the greatest threat to the other surviving kingdoms which sought to form an alliance to stem Qin's growing power. The various commanders of the empire gathered in the formerly powerful state of Zhou to plan an attack on Qin. King Chao Xiong of Qin was concerned about the gathering of warlords when his minister, Marquis Ying, said, "Allow me to get rid of them. Qin has no quarrel with these 'commanders of the empire.' They gather now to make plans for an attack against Qin simply because each seeks wealth and fame for himself. Look at your own hounds—some are sleeping, some are up, some walk about and others are sim-

1. For directions on who is vulnerable to this strategy the following quote from Du Mu is appropriate:

"Among the official class there are worthy men who have been deprived of office; others who have committed errors and have been punished. There are sycophants and minions who are covetous of wealth. There are those who wrongly remain long in lowly office; those who have not obtained responsible positions, and those whose sole desire is to take advantage of times of trouble to extend the scope of their own abilities. There are those who are two-faced, changeable, and deceitful, and who are always sitting on the fence. With these you can secretly inquire after their welfare, reward them liberally with gold and silk, and so tie them to you. Then you may rely on them to seek out the real facts of the situation in their country, and to ascertain its plans directed against you. They can as well create cleavages between the sovereign and his ministers so that these are not in harmonious accord."

ply standing where they are. But throw a bone to them and they will all be on their feet in an instant, snapping at each other. Why? You have given them a reason to fight each other."

The king understood and asked the minister to continue. Minister Ying called in another official and said, "We must dispatch Tang Chu complete with musicians and five thousand in gold to set up quarters in Wu An. There he will send out a proclamation addressed to all military commanders saying that whoever wishes to defect to Qin will be given a sumptuous banquet and generous gifts of money. But those who conspire against Qin will receive nothing." Minister Ying turned to Tang Chu and said, "In order to succeed you must not care where the money goes, but insure that you distribute all of it. Once the money is gone we will send another five thousand taels!" A few days after Tang Chu left with the gold, he sent a report saying that he was able to distribute only three thousands pieces of gold before all the commanders of the empire took to fighting amongst themselves to see who would claim the greater reward. Needless to say they were unable to cooperate and no alliance against Qin was formed. For the next thirty years Qin continue to sow discord between the remaining states. Their constant bickering and infighting prevented them from ever uniting against their common enemy. Qin conquered them one by one until none remained.[2]

THREE KINGDOMS PERIOD CHINA

Cao Cao, the warlord of Wei, was on campaign against a rival commander Zhou Yu. Cao Cao won several battles and chased his enemy south into an area of rivers, lakes, and marshes. Coming from the northern plains of Wei, Cao's troops were unaccustomed to naval combat and suffered their first defeat at the hands of Zhou. Cao

2. From the ZHAN GUO CE.

Cao made camp beside the river and began constructing an armada while retraining his troops in naval tactics. To this end he hired the services of two renowned naval commanders who came from the south. During this time one of Cao Cao's advisors, Jiang Kan, offered another plan. Since Jiang was a former friend of Zhou Yu, he would go to try and talk him into surrendering and joining with Wei. Cao Cao agreed to the plan and Jiang was given a small boat and an oarsman to paddle him up river to Zhou Yu's camp. Zhou Yu guessed right away Jiang's real purpose and played in turn the tactic of the "doomed spy."[3] Zhou Yu treated Jian like a long lost brother and arranged a celebration of food and wine. During the feasting, Zhou Yu slipped out and gave instructions to his attendants to forge two letters and place them on his desk. During the festivities, Jiang tried to persuade Zhou Yu to join forces with him, but Zhou Yu feigned drunkenness to avoid the subject. Later Zhou Yu invited his friend to share his quarters, and shortly after retiring he pretended to pass out. For a while Jiang also pretended to sleep, but after making sure his host was asleep, Jiang silently crept about the room to see what he could find. He discovered the two letters and was intrigued to read about a plan to betray Cao Cao in the next battle. More shocking was that the letters were signed by Wei's new naval commanders. Jiang quickly hid the letters in his robe. Early the next morning he made his apologies and left before Zhou Yu awoke. When he arrived back at Cao Cao's camp he reported that his mission had been a failure, but it wasn't a complete loss since he had some intelligence concerning a plot to stage a palace coup. He then produced

---

3. As recounted in Sun Zi's The Art of War, Chapter 13, a "doomed spy" is one whom you allow to witness staged events so that they will convincingly file a false report. After the ruse is discovered those spies are usually executed for incompetence, hence the term "doomed."

the forged letters. After reading the documents Cao Cao had the two naval commanders executed. In this way Zhou Yu removed Cao Cao's two best assets in naval warfare. When Cao Cao launched a naval attack months later he suffered a terrible defeat and barely escaped with his life (see Chapter 34).[4]

SIX DYNASTIES PERIOD CHINA

During the later Wei dynasty, the emperor Tai Wu led a hundred thousand troops against the Song general Zang Zhi. The emperor, with his superior forces, chased general Zhang to the city of Yu where he was cornered. The city was strongly fortified, and so the emperor planned to surround it and starve the defenders into surrender. Feeling confident of his position, the emperor sent a cart carrying a large jar of wine to the city gate with the message asking for the traditional exchange of wine before commencing his siege of the city. Zang Zhi, knowing that he needed to fight a decisive battle quickly or suffer defeat, saw this as an opportunity. He sent some soldiers to gratefully accept the jar of wine and in turn deliver another large jar sealed with the wine maker's stamp. When a cup of this wine was poured for the emperor it was discovered to be urine. This caused the emperor a humiliating loss of face before his own troops, and, in a rage, he ordered an immediate assault on the city. The defenders were well prepared and the bodies of the slain imperial troops piled up nearly to the top of the ramparts. In his haste and anger the emperor lost half his forces.[5]

---

4. From ROMANCE OF THE THREE KINGDOMS.

5. From the LI ZHUAN.

SUMMARY

A person's ability to function effectively is dependent on being in harmony with one's environment. By disrupting your enemy's environment, you disrupt his harmony, thus interfering with his ability to attack or defend.

第三十四計

CHAPTER THIRTY-FOUR

苦肉計

THE STRATEGY OF INJURING YOURSELF

To be the first to gain victory, initially display some weakness to the enemy and only afterward do battle. Then your effort will be half, but the achievement doubled.
—THE SIX SECRET TEACHINGS OF THE TAI GONG

Pretending to be injured has two possible applications. In the first, the enemy is lulled into relaxing his guard since he no longer considers you to be an immediate threat. The second is a way of ingratiating yourself to your enemy by pretending the injury was caused by a mutual enemy.

THREE KINGDOMS PERIOD CHINA

During the last days of the crumbling Han empire the renowned general Sun Ce was on campaign against a rival province. He had chased the enemy to the walled city of Moling where they were holed up. Sun knew it would be too costly to attack fortified positions, so he attempted to arouse the enemy's anger by parading up and down the city walls hurling insults at the defenders. But the commander of the city, Xue Li, refused to come out to fight despite the taunts. One day while Sun was out riding, a soldier on the city wall shot an arrow which hit Sun in the thigh, only slightly penetrating his armor. Sun rode back to camp where he was treated for a flesh wound. However, rumors were spreading that the general had been mortally wounded. The commanders thought he should go out of his tent to reassure the troops, but Sun used the situation to play a stratagem. He let it be known that he was mortally wounded and had his soldiers pretend to prepare for a funeral ceremony. Hearing that Sun Ce was dead, Xue Li saw this as his chance and rushed his army out to attack the camp. Sun Ce's troops pretended to retreat leading the attackers into an ambush that closed in from four directions with Sun charging out on his horse to the shouts of "Sun Ce lives!" The shocked city garrison threw down their arms and surrendered while Xue Li and a few loyal guards were slain trying to escape.[1]

EDO PERIOD JAPAN

During the Tokugawa period Kaei Juzo, a former spy, had come under suspicion and was in danger of being assassinated. It turned out that the man sent to kill him was a former acquaintance called Tonbe. Not wishing to kill his old friend, Tonbe and Juzo worked out the classic ploy as follows. Tonbe brought Juzo back as a pris-

---

1. From ROMANCE OF THE THREE KINGDOMS.

oner to the Shogun. Juzo begged the Shogun to allow him one last dignity: permission to commit *seppuku*.[2] The Shogun, curious to see the notorious spy's bravery in death, allowed him that privilege. Juzo was given a dagger which he plunged into his belly, and, cutting sideways, he spilled his intestines onto the ground before falling over. The guards removed the body and threw it in the castle's moat. A short time later Juzo quietly swum to shore and escaped the district. Knowing that his warrior's reputation would merit him the right of committing *seppuku*, Juzo had strapped a dead fox across his abdomen, when the fox's intestines spilled out it was indistinguishable from human intestines.[3]

THREE KINGDOMS PERIOD CHINA

Zhou Yu was the chief advisor for the state of Wu, which was at war with the powerful kingdom of Wei lead by the warlord Cao Cao. Cao Cao had sent two spies posing as defectors over to the Wu capital but Zhou Yu spotted them immediately. Rather than have the spies executed, Zhou Yu again used the tactic of the "doomed spy" (see Chapter 33). Zhou Yu sent for his senior and most trusted naval commander, Huang Gai, and together they devised a strategy. The next day at court Huang started an argument with Zhou Yu that escalated to the point where Zhou Yu ordered the naval commander's execution. Horrified at the prospect of losing one of their ablest commanders, the other court advisors intervened on Huang's behalf. Reluctantly, Zhou Yu commuted the sentence to fifty strokes of a staff to be carried out in the town square. This punishment was often fatal in itself, and the Wei spies who watched the beating were convinced that Huang Gai

---

2. An extremely painful form of ritual suicide in which a dagger is used to cut across the lower belly.

3. From THE WAY OF THE NINJA.

and Zhou Yu had truly fallen out. The next day, while still recovering from the ordeal, Huang secretly sent a message to the Wei camp offering to defect. At first Cao Cao was suspicious, but when he called in his spies they confirmed seeing Huang beaten to near death in the city square. Cao Cao was in desperate need for an able naval commander (having recently executed his top two admirals on suspicions of treachery), so he gave the order to have Huang smuggled into his camp. After the usual formalities Cao Cao asked for Huang Gai's advice on how to train his land based infantry in naval warfare. Huang Gai said, "Since the men of Wei are used to fighting on solid earth we should make the war junks as stable as the earth. Your lordship has a great number of boats, and if we had them strung together with chains, and the gaps between the boats covered over with planking, then it would be as stable as land." Cao Cao agreed to the plan, and after weeks of construction the huge floating platform proved so stable that the Wei soldiers felt like they were walking on solid ground. When Zhou Yu's spies reported Cao Cao's new naval strategy he was ready to attack. The next day, some say by divine intervention, the winds changed direction enabling Zhou Yu to send fire ships down-wind against the floating island of Wei. When Cao Cao felt the change in wind direction[4] and saw the burning ships bearing down, he knew all was lost. The minute one of his ships caught fire the whole fleet was doomed since, being chained together, no ship could escape. The entire Wei armada was completely destroyed and Cao Cao himself barely escaped with a handful of troops.[5]

---

4. Cao Cao was no fool and knew of his armada's vulnerability to an attack by fire. But he had counted on the seasonal winds to remain blowing in a constant direction. It was the knowledge that at that time of year there would be a sudden change in wind direction that Zhou Yu had counted on when devising this strategy.

5. From ROMANCE OF THE THREE KINGDOMS.

SUMMARY

The tactic of feigning injury to lower your opponent's guard or avoid aggression is so universally applied that it is even found among many species of birds, fish, and animals. The principle is simple: if your are sick or injured, you are less of a threat.

連環計

THE STRATEGY OF COMBINING TACTICS

Do not repeat tactics which gained you victory in the past, but let your tactics be molded by the infinite variety of circumstances.

—SUN ZI

Appearance and intention inevitably ensnare people when artfully used, even if people sense that there is an ulterior intention behind the overt appearance. When you set up ploys and opponents fall for them, then you win by letting them act on your ruse. As for those who do not fall for a ploy, when you see they won't fall into one trap, you have another set. Then even if opponents haven't fallen for your original ploy, in effect they actually have.

—YAGYU MUNENORI,
FAMILY BOOK ON THE ART OF WAR

In important matters one should use several strategies applied simultaneously. Keep different plans operating in an overall scheme. In this manner if any one strategy fails you would still have several others to fall back on. Combining even weak strategies in unison has a greater effectiveness than applying them sequentially.

WARRING STATES PERIOD CHINA

The heir of Chu, Qing Xiong, was a hostage at the court of Qi when news came of his father's death. He asked permission from the king of Qi to return home to attend the funeral. The king replied, "If we are given five hundred *li* of your eastern lands you will be allowed to return. If you refuse you will stay here." Qing Xiong agreed to cede the land for his freedom and was allowed to return to Chu and become its new king. Shortly thereafter an envoy of fifty chariots arrived from Qi demanding to take possession of the territory. The king of Chu summoned his top three generals one after the other and asked each in turn for their recommendations. The first general said, "The king has no recourse but to give up the land. From a king must come only the truth. To have promised something and failed to give it would be a breach of faith. Thereafter no one will ever trust your promise. I submit that you give them the land to show your good faith, then attack Qi and fight to get it back, which would show your valor."

The second general was asked for his opinion and he said, "You cannot give it back. What makes a country strong is the land. To give five hundred *li* is to lose almost half our country. I ask to be allowed to go out and defend the eastern boarder."

Then the third general was called in and he said, "You cannot give them the land, yet we are not powerful enough to defend it alone. I beg permission to go west and seek aid from Qin."

After hearing the counsel of his three advisors the king consulted his minister Shen Ci asking which of the three strategies he should follow. Shen Ci said, "Use them all! Let each general carry out his own strategy unbeknownst to the others and we shall see which prevails."

So the next day the king sent the first general to meet the envoy from Qi and surrender the territory. The day after that he commissioned the second general to go defend the eastern border. On the third day he sent the third general to Qin with a plea for aid. The first general rode out to the eastern territory to rendezvous with the envoy from Qi who had come to take possession of the territory. The next day they were intercepted en route by the second general who told the envoy from Qi that he had mustered troops to defend the territory. The envoy turned to the first general and asked, "You have come to surrender the territory, but now we have another general to defend it. How can this be?" The first general replied, "I was personally instructed by the king in this matter. This man is usurping his authority and he should be attacked." The Qi envoy sent for reinforcements and when they arrived a few days later they were led by the king himself. Just as they were about to form battle lines the third general arrived with a relief force from Qin. The Qin general called out to the king of Qi, "To have detained the heir of Chu was wicked, and to rob him of five hundred *li* of his eastern lands is unjust. If you wish to withdraw your troops you may. If not, then you must contend with us as well." The king of Qi was frightened by this unexpected turn of events and quietly retreated. The king of Chu thus saved both his territory and his reputation.[1]

WARRING STATES PERIOD CHINA

In 284 B.C. the state of Yan attacked and defeated Qi. The remaining Qi forces under the command of Tian Dan fled to the city of Jimo for a final stand. The renowned Yan general Yue Yi had surrounded the city when the news came that the king of Yan had died and was succeeded by Prince Hui. Years earlier, when the prince was still heir apparent, he and general Yue had numerous clashes and disagreements. When Tian Dan heard the news he sent secret agents to the new king to spread rumors that Yue Yi was planning to revolt because he feared being executed for past disagreements. When Prince Hui heard this rumor he sent another general to replace Yue Yi who fled to another state. The replacement general, Qi Che, was a brash and arrogant up-start who began reissuing orders and procedures which merely succeeded in causing confusion and dissension among the officers.

Next, Tian Dan had the womenfolk line the city walls and beg for a peaceful surrender while he sent gold and treasure collected from the city's wealthiest citizens to general Qi Che with a note asking that the women and children be spared in return for the peaceful surrender of the city. These events convinced Qi Che that the city was truly about to capitulate, and he allowed his troops to relax their guard. After this careful preparation Tian Dan felt the time was right to launch his counter attack. First, he had the citizens of the city gather with drums and cooking pots and instructed them that on a signal they were to make as much noise as possible. He then had breaches made

---

1. From the ZHAN GUO CE.

along the city walls from the inside. Next, a herd of cattle was painted in bizarre patterns and knives and sickles tied to their horns and torches tied to their tails. Just before daylight three events occurred in rapid succession. The citizens within the city struck up a cacophony of noise which startled the sleeping Yan troops. Then the torches on the tails of the cattle were lit and they were released through the breaches in the wall. The enraged animals ran madly about the Yen camp killing stunned troops with their horns and setting fire to tents with their tails. Then Qi's crack troops rushed out from the gates to attack the now terrified and utterly confused troops. Tian Dan defeated the Yan army and went on to conquer more than seventy cities.[2]

HEIAN PERIOD JAPAN

In 1183, in what would be called the battle of Kurikara, Taira Koremori of the ruling Taira clan led a hundred thousand troops east to attack Minamoto Yoshinaka of the rebel Minamoto clan. To enter the Minamoto territory the Taira would have to cross Japan's central mountain range at its northern end where the mountains were little more than large hills. There was only one pass that an army the size of the Taira's could use—Kurikara pass. Traveling east through the pass one would see near the other side an open valley that appeared to cut through the mountain, but in fact the valley narrowed down into a box canyon. Seeking to take advantage of this unusual terrain, Yoshinaka devised the following strategies. First, he needed to buy time, so he sent a detachment of troops to occupy a small hill down-slope of the Taira advance. These troops carried extra flags which they planted on the hill to make it appear that a large host was stationed there. The next day the Minamoto sta-

2. From RECORDS OF THE GRAND HISTORIAN.

tioned on the hill challenged the Taira to battle according to all the ancient samurai protocols, to which the Taira readily complied. First, there was an archery duel using humming bulb arrows, then sharp point arrows, then individual duels, and finally a skirmish of a hundred cavalry each. While all this gentlemanly warfare was being fought, Yoshinaka had sent another detachment of troops through the forest to quietly set up positions to the rear of the Taira. By nightfall the Taira were about to retire when two events occurred. First, the hidden Minamoto troops launched a sudden attack from the rear, while the troops on the hill charged down to join the first group. This sudden attack caused the Taira to retreat down the pass, but at this point the second event occurred. Yoshinaka had earlier confiscated a herd of cattle and had torches tied to their horns. The torches were set on fire and the enraged animals were released so that they charged up through the pass towards the retreating Taira.[3] The bizarre spectacle of the enraged and fiery beasts charging through the pass caused complete panic among the Taira troops who saw their only avenue of escape to be down the side of the pass and into the valley. In the darkness the troops scrambled down the steep slopes and on through the valley, many being killed in falls. When the first of the fleeing soldiers reached the box end they attempted to turn back, but those in front were crushed by the weight of their own troops who kept piling in, not yet realizing they were trapped. Yoshinaka then launched his final tactic and sent his main body of troops into the valley after the fleeing Taira. The slaughter was horrendous, with over seventy thousand Taira soldiers killed.

3. Chinese works of strategy and espionage were popular readings among the samurai commanders, and it was quite probable that Yoshinaka got the idea of tying torches to the bulls from reading the account of Tian Dan.

Yoshinaka was killed in a later battle, but the Minamoto clan eventually succeeded in wiping out the Taira ruling elite in 1185. The Minamoto held power for only thirty years before they too were toppled from power.[4]

SUMMARY

To insure victory one must know how to launch simultaneous attacks. Both from left, and from right; from the outside, and from within; from above, and from below. Advantage goes to those who can attack on several fronts; disadvantage to those who must defend against more than one.

---

4. From THE SAMURAI.

CHAPTER THIRTY-SIX

第三十六計

走爲上

IF ALL ELSE FAILS,
RETREAT

If greatly outnumbered, then retreat. While it is possible for a small force to put up a great fight, in the end it will lose to superior numbers.
—SUN ZI

If it becomes obvious that your current course of action will lead to defeat, then retreat and regroup. When your side is losing, there are only three choices remaining: surrender, compromise, or escape. Surrender is complete defeat, compromise is half defeat, but escape is not defeat. As long as you are not defeated, you still have a chance.[1]

---

1. When faced with more powerful opponents, apply guerrilla tactics: attack, retreat, and evade. A large body of men expends greater

SPRING AND AUTUMN PERIOD CHINA

In 597 B.C. the states of Chu and Jin fought the battle of Bi. For days before the battle the two armies faced each other, unsure whether or not a battle would actually take place. Several small skirmishes were fought to release the energies of the officers, but it appeared that a peace treaty would be negotiated instead. On the Jin side the commander of the left wing, Shi Hui, advised caution saying, "It would be well to take precautions. If Chu has no hostile intent, then we can do away with the precautions and conclude an alliance. But if Chu should come charging down on us, the precautions will prevent our defeat. Even when the Lords come together at a meeting, they take care not to dismiss their personal bodyguards." But the commander of the main body, Xian Gu, disagreed, and only Shi Hui took the precaution of stationing troops in ambush near his positions. The next day, during a small skirmish, the Chu forces misunderstood the commotion for an attack by Jin and launched a full scale assault. The Chu charged forth with such speed and determination that the Jin lines collapsed from the impact. Another Chu division made ready to attack the Jin left wing commanded by Shi Hui. An officer rode up to Shi Hui and asked, "Should we wait for their attack?"

Shi Hui replied, "The Chu army is now at the peak of its vigor. If they make a concerted attack on us, our army is bound to be wiped out! Better to gather up our forces and quit the field. Though we will still share the disgrace with the other divisions, we at least spare the

---

energy in pursuit than a small force does in flight. A small group of guerrillas can move faster, especially through difficult terrain, and can forage off their environment for short term survival needs, whereas the larger group moves slower through difficult terrain and is also susceptible to logistical problems. The longer the chase continues, the longer their supply lines and the greater the cost.

lives of our men. Is that not the best that could be had from this situation?"

Shi Hui had the men stationed in ambush fight a rear guard action, enabling him to retreat with almost his entire division intact. The main Jin troops suffered a resounding defeat with heavy casualties. Commander Xian Gu, who had so thoughtlessly disregarded the advice to take precautions, was found guilty of incompetence and executed.[2]

WARRING STATES PERIOD CHINA

When Wang Chu was hostage in Yan the king wanted him executed, and so he fled. While trying to cross the border he was captured by a border guard.

"The king of Yan wants me killed," said Wang Chu to the guard, "because someone told him I have a pearl of great value and he wants it. In truth, I lost it long ago, but the king refuses to believe me. If you turn me in I shall say that you took the pearl from me and swallowed it. Your king will have you killed and turn you entrails inside out to find it. If you want to turn me over to your ruler I cannot dissuade you by offering you anything, but remember, if I am taken, it is your vitals which will be chopped to pieces." The guard promptly let Chu go.[3]

MING DYNASTY CHINA

The Ming emperor Huidi had disposed of all his uncles except one who feigned madness (see Chapter 27). In 1403 this very uncle, the prince of Yan, led a huge army to the capital of Nanjing to seize the throne. The city was surrounded and the emperor was considering suicide when he was stopped by a eunuch who told him that his grandfather, Emperor Hong Wu, had left a

---

2. From the ZHAN GUO CE, Watson edition.

3. Ibid.

chest in his care with orders that, should any great crisis occur to threaten the dynasty, the reigning emperor should open the chest.

"Let us open it at once then," said the emperor, "and see what my grandfather would do were he here now." When the lid was lifted the box was found to contain the robes of a Buddhist monk, a diploma, a razor, and ten ingots of silver. The emperor understood the meaning at once and with a handful of attendants fled the palace through a secret tunnel to a Buddhist temple. There he shaved his head and put on the robes. He made his way out of the city and all the way to Sichuan province where he lived in obscurity in a remote monastery.

Meanwhile the palace had burned down during the fighting and it was assumed that the emperor had died in the fire. Forty years later during the rein of emperor Ying Zong (the fourth since Huidi's time), an old Buddhist priest arrived at court and claimed to be the old emperor Huidi. It turned out the man was an impostor, but a rumor began that Huidi was still alive. To quell the rumors and settle the issue, an official investigation was made which discovered that Huidi was indeed still alive and living as a Buddhist priest. The old emperor was invited back to the capital with great ceremony and he lived out his last days as a guest in the palace. However, he was kept under a watchful eye.[4]

SUMMARY

The ancient Daoist sages invented the principle of "non-action," or "following the course of the times." To not take advantage of an opportunity presented is a violation of this principle. Conversely, to fight a battle that cannot be won is an equal violation of heaven's law. In the art of war an often overlooked but vital talent is knowing when to run.

---

4. From IMPERIAL HISTORY OF CHINA.

CHRONOLOGICAL TABLES

CHINA

Xia Dynasty	2205-1776 B.C.
Shang Dynasty	1766-1122
Zhou Dynasty	1122-256
Spring & Autumn Period	771-481
Warring States Period	403-221
Qin Dynasty	221-297
Han Dynasty	221 B.C.-A.D. 220
Three Kingdoms	220-280
Six Dynasties	222-589
Sui Dynasty	589-618
Tang	618-907
Five Dynasties	907-959
Song Dynasty	960-1126
Yuan Dynasty	1279-1368
Ming Dynasty	1368-1644
Qing Dynasty	1644-1911

JAPAN

Legendary Era	?-645
Nara	646-793
Heian	794-1184
Kamakura	1185-1367
Muromachi	1368-1575
Momoyama	1576-1614
Edo	1615-1867

BIBLIOGRAPHY

Alexander, Bevin.
How Great Generals Win. W.W. Norton & Co., New York, 1993.

Alexander, William, and Mason, George Henry.
Views of 18th Century China. Studio Editions, London, 1988 (First published 1804-5).

Bingham, Woodbridge.
The Founding of the T'ang Dynasty. Octagon Books, New York, 1975.

Birch, Cyril, Editor.
Anthology Of Chinese Literature: From Early Ttimes to the Fourteenth Century. Grove Press, New York, 1965.

Blumenson, Martin, and Stokesbury, James L.
Masters of the Art of Command. Da Capo, Boston, 1975.

Chesneaux, Jean.
Popular Movements and Secret Societies in China, 1840-1950. Stanford University Press, California, 1972.

Cleary, Thomas.
The Japanese Art Of War: Understanding the Culture of Strategy. Shambala Publications, Boston, 1991.

Cleary, Thomas.
Mastering the Art of War: Zhuge Liang's and Liu Ji's Commentaries on the Classic by Sun Tzu. Shambala Publications, Boston, 1989.

Cleary, Thomas.
The Lost Art Of War: Sun Bin's Art of War. HarperSanFrancisco, 1996.

Crump, J. J., Jr., Translator.
Chan-Kuo Ts'e (Intrigues of the Warring States). Clarendon Press, Oxford, 1970.

Daraul, Arkon.
A History of Secret Societies. Citadel Press, New York, 1990.

De Lacouperie, Terrien.
Western Origin of the Early Chinese Civilization, From 2,300 B.C. To 200 A.D. Osnabruck, Otto Zeller, 1966. (First published 1894).

Deshimaru, Taisen.
The Zen Way to the Martial Arts. E.P. Dutton, New York, 1982.

Draeger, Donn F.
Ninjitsu, The Art of Invisibility. Yen books, Japan, 1989.

Dun J. Li.
The Essence Of Chinese Civilization. D. Van Nostrand, Princeton, 1967.

Dunnigan, James F., and Bay, Austin.
A Quick and Dirty Guide to War. William Morrow, New York, 1991.

Dunnigan, James F.
How To Make War. William Morrow, New York, 1988.

Fang, Achilles.
The Chronicle of the Three Kingdoms. Cambridge University
Press, 1952.

Fang Hsuan-ling. Rogers, Michael C., Translator.
The Chronicle of Fu Chien. University of California Press,
Berkeley, 1968.

Farris, William Wayne.
*Heavenly Warriors: The Evolution of Japan's Military 500-
1300.* Harvard University Press, 1992.

Friday, Karl F.
*Hired Swords: The Rise of Private Warrior Power in Early
Japan.* Stanford University Press, California, 1992.

Gardner, C. S.
Chinese Traditional Historiography. Cambridge University
Press, 1938.

Griffith, Samual B.
Sun Tzu, The Art of War. Oxford University Press, 1963.

Heider, John.
The Tao Of Leadership. Bantam Books, New York, 1986.

Hiroaki, Sato, Translator.
The Sword and The Mind. Overlook Press, New York,
1985.

Hiroaki, Sato, Translator.
Legends of the Samurai. Overlook Press, New York, 1995.

Kierman, Frank A., Editor.
Chinese Ways in Warfare. Harvard University Press,
Cambridge, 1974.

Johnston, Alastair Iain.
*Cultural Realism, Strategic Culture and Grand Strategy in Chinese
History.* Princeton University Press, Princeton, 1995.

Koh Kok Kiang, and Liu Yi.
The Secret Art of War: Thirty Six Stratagems. Asiapac,
Singapore, 1992.

Lao Tzu.
Tao Te Ching. Penguin Classics, New York, 1963.

Lau, Theodora.
Best-Loved Chinese Proverbs. Harper Perennial, New York,
1995.

Legge, James, Translator.
*The Chinese Classics: Vol. V, The Ch'un Ts'ew with The Tso
Chuan (Spring and Autumn Annals).* Oxford University
Press, Shanghai, 1935.

Legge, James, Translator.
*The Chinese Classics: Vol. III, The Shoo King or Book of
Historical Documents.* Oxford University Press, Shanghai,
1935.

Lewis, Mark Edward.
Sanctioned Violence in Early China. State University of
New York Press, New York, 1990.

Li Yu-ning.
The First Emperor of China. ISAP, White Plains, 1975.

Lo Kuan-Chung. Moss Roberts, Translator.
Romance of the Three Kingdoms. Pantheon Books, New
York, 1976.

Liu I-Ch'ing. Mather, Richard B., Translator.
Shih-shuo Hsin-yu, A New Account of Tales of the World.
University of Minnesota Press, Minneapolis, 1976.

Ma Senliang.
*Sanshiliu Ji Gu Jin Yin Li. (The Thirty-six Strategies with
Examples from Times Past and Present).* Starite Book Co.,
Hong Kong, 1985.

Ma, Y. W., and Lau, Joseph S. M.
Traditional Chinese Stories. Columbia University Press, New York, 1978.

McNeilly, Mark.
Sun Tzu and the Art of Business. Oxford Press, New York, 1996.

Macgowan, J.
The Imperial History of China. Curzon Press, New York, 1973. (First published 1897).

Machiavelli, Niccolo.
The Prince. Bantam Book Classics, New York, 1985.

Morris, Ivan.
The Nobility of Failure: Tragic Heroes in the History of Japan. The Noonday Press, New York, 1975.

Murray, Williamson, with MacGregor Knox and Alvin Bernstein.
The Making of Strategy, Rulers, States, and War. Cambridge University Press, 1994.

Murray, Dianne H., and Qin Baoqi.
The Origins of the Tiandihui: The Chinese Triads in Legend and History. Stanford University Press, California, 1994.

Miyamoto, Musashi.
The Book Of Five Rings. Bantam Books, New York, 1982.

Needham, Joseph.
Science and Civilization in China, Vol. II: History of Scientific Thought. Cambridge Press, 1954.

Nicolle, David.
The Mongol Warlords. Firebird Books, Dorset, England, 1990.

Ong Hean-Tatt.
The Chinese Pakua: An Expose. Pelanduk Publishers, Malaysia, 1991.

Ownby, David.
Brotherhoods and Secret Societies in Early and Mid-Qing China.
Stanford University Press, California, 1996.

Ownby, David, Editor.
Secret Societies Reconsidered: Perspectives on the Social History of Modern South Asia and Southeast Asia. M.E. Sharpe, Armonk, 1993.

Palmer, M., and Breuilly, E., Translators.
The Book of Chuang Tzu. Arkana, London, 1996.

Pan, Lynn.
Sons of The Yellow Emperor: A History of the Chinese Diaspora.
Little, Brown & Company, Boston, 1990.

Pan K'u. Homer H. Dubs, Translator.
History of the Former Han Dynasty (Han Shu), Vol. I-II.
Waverly Press, Baltimore, 1938.

Pan K'u. Clyde Bailey Sargent, Translator.
Wang Mang. Hyperion Books, Westport, Connecticut, 1977.

Phillipi, Donald L., Translator.
Kojiki (Record of Ancient Things). University of Tokyo Press, Japan, 1968.

Piggott, Juliet.
Japanese Mythology. Peter Bedrick Books, New York, 1969.

Reps, Paul.
Zen Flesh, Zen Bones. Doubleday, New York, 1972.

Roberts, J.A.G.
A History of China: Prehistory to c.1800. St. Martin's Press, New York, 1996.

Roberts, Moss.
Chinese Tales & Fantasies. Pantheon Books, New York, 1979.

Sage, Steven.
Ancient Sichuan and the Unification of China. State University of New York Press, New York, 1992.

Sansom, George.
A History Of Japan, 1334–1615. Stanford University Press, California, 1961.

Sawyer, Ralph D., Translator.
The Seven Military Classics of Ancient China. Westview Press, Boulder, 1993.

Sawyer, Ralph D., Translator.
Unorthodox Strategies for the Everyday Warrior. Westview Press, Boulder, 1996.

Sawyer, Ralph D., Translator.
The Complete Art of War, Sun Tzu, Sun Pin. Westview Press, Boulder, 1996.

Schlegel, Gustave.
The Hung League. Lang & Co., Batavia, 1866. (Reprinted by AMS New York, 1973.)

Shu Han.
Sanshiliu Ji Miben Jijie, (The Secret Book of the Thirty-six Strategies, with Explanations). National Press, Taipei, 1986.

Sun Tzu. Roger T. Ames, Translator.
The Art of War. Ballantine Books, New York, 1993.

Sun Tzu. Clavell, James, Editor.
The Art of War. Delacorte Press, New York, 1983.

Sun Pin. D. C. Lau and Roger T. Ames, Translators.
The Art of Warfare. Ballantine Books, New York, 1996.

Takuan Soho. Wilson, William Scott, Translator.
The Unfettered Mind: Writings of the Zen Master to the Sword Master. Kodansha International, Tokyo, 1986.

Teng, S. Y.
The Nien Army and Their Guerrilla Warfare 1851-1868. Paris
Mouton & Co, The Hague, Netherlands, 1961.

Turnbull, Stephen.
The Samurai, A Military History. Osprey Publishing,
London, 1977.

Turnbull, Stephen.
Samurai Warriors. Blandford, London, 1987.

Von Senger, Harro. Myron B. Gubitz, Translator.
The Book of Strategems. Viking Press, New York, 1991.

Waltham, Clae.
Shu Ching: Book of History. Henry Regnery, Chicago,
1971.

Wang Gungwu.
*The Structure of Power in North China During the Five
Dynasties.* University of Malaya Press, 1963.

Ward, J.S.M.
The Hung Society Vol. I-III. The Baskerville Press,
London, 1926.

Watson, Burton, Translator.
Records of the Grand Historian of China, (Shih Chi).
Columbia University Press, New York, 1961.

Watson, Burton, Translator.
The Tso Chuan. Columbia University Press, 1989.

Wechsler, Howard J.
*Mirror to the Son of Heaven, Wei Cheng at the Court of T'ang
T'ai-tsung.* Yale University Press, 1974.

Williamson, H. R.
Wang An Shih, Vol. I-II. Hyperion, Connecticut, 1935.

Wright, Arthur E..
The Sui Dynasty. Alfred A. Knopf, New York, 1978.

Yang Liyi.
100 *Chinese Idioms and Their Stories*. Beijing Commercial Press, Beijing, 1991.

Yu Hsiu Sen.
Ancient Chinese Parables. The Commercial Press, Shanghai, 1924.

Zou Zongxu. Susan Whitfield, Translator.
The Land Within The Passes: A History of Xian. Viking Press, London, 1987.

The Best Source
of Infomation
from and about
China
Since 1960.

www.chinabooks.com